¡Tequila!

Cooking with the Spirit of Mexico

Un Brindis Mexicano:
¡Salud, amor y dinero
y el tiempo para gozarlo!

A Mexican Toast:
Health, wealth, and romance
and the time to enjoy them all!

¡TEQUILA!

Cooking with the Spirit of Mexico

Lucinda Hutson

Illustrations by Julie Marshall

10 TEN SPEED PRESS

TEN SPEED PRESS
P.O. Box 7123
Berkeley, CA 94707

Cover and text design by Fifth Street Design, Berkeley CA
Cover and interior illustration by Julie Marshall

Library of Congress Cataloging-in-Publication Data:
Hutson, Lucinda, 1950-
    Tequila!: cooking the spirit of Mexico / Lucinda Hutson; illustrations
  by Julie Marshall.
       p.   cm.
    Includes index.
    ISBN 0-89815-564-9: $24.95. — ISBN 0-89815-663-7 (pbk.): $16.95
    1. Tequila.   2. Pulque.   3. Mescal.   I. Marshall, Julia.
II. Title.
TP807. T46H88   1994
641.2'5—dc20   94-29104
                                                              CIP

First Printing 1995
Printed in Hong Kong
1   2   3   4   5 — 98   97   96   95

"Calavera Borracho"
Drunken Skeleton...
wood cut by Posada

I SURVIVED TEQUILAFEST

Toma tequila,
mas no dejes que la tequila
tome a ti.

Drink tequila,
but don't let tequila
consume you.

Table of Contents

List of Recipes

About the artwork

My home is filled with Mexican folk art—souvenirs from my travels south of the border. Many of the artists who created these pieces are personal friends, making the collection even more meaningful to me. To illustrate this book, I have taken these *tesoros* (or treasures) down from my shelves and used them as "artist's models." In this way, they have been brought to life in lively watercolor renditions. For me, each painting created expressly for *¡Tequila!* evokes a memory of Mexico, a colorful reminder of the people and country that have so greatly influenced my life. I also have collected *dichos* (traditional Mexican proverbs), and have used them to further embellish this book.

I thank Julie Marshall for her beautiful watercolor paintings. They capture the spirit of the original folk art. In keeping with the theme of this book, we have at times taken artistic license, slightly altering the original folk art with some whimsy, such as adding a bottle of tequila into the hands of the carved mermaid, who in my home holds a fish instead.

Mexico has given much richness to my life. In return, my *gracias* is to help preserve in these pages some of the disappearing expressions of her rich and ancient culture: folk art, proverbs, and recipes. In doing so, I also offer you a glimpse into the soul of the country that stole my heart years ago.

The discovery of tequila (detail) **painted by Gabriel Flores hung at La Perseverancia, the Sauza distillery**

INTRODUCTION

Tequila is my soulmate: Mexico in a bottle, its flavor is as melodic to the mouth as a mariachi tune to the ear—bold, spicy, and full of life! Upon the first taste, it gives a liquid jolt to the senses that makes our tongues trill, trumpets resound in our ears, and throatily bellowed—ay-ay-ay! *gritos* fill the air. Tequila makes *macho* men burst into passionate lyrics of unrequited love and shy women dance on tables.

My affinity for tequila seems to be a natural one, a legacy from my West Texas hometown of El Paso, a border town steeped in three noteworthy events in tequila's history: (1) the first three barrels of tequila imported into the United States passed through El Paso in 1873; (2) the first margarita may have been poured in a bar in nearby Juárez in 1942; and (3) it was there that I first learned how to drink tequila.

When I was growing up, good food and fun were always found in Juárez, on the Mexican side of the border near El Paso, and *cantinas* bustled there on Saturday nights. While my companions guzzled Singapore Slings and Zombies—dreadful concoctions that promised speedy inebriation—I would slip into the kitchen of our favorite *cantina*. Tío Mauro Orozco, the uncle of my family's housekeeper, was the cook. He would pour me a shot of silver tequila, and with *ranchera* music blaring on the radio to the rhythmic patting of tortillas, I learned how to cook and how to drink tequila. Meanwhile, my amigos unwittingly imbibed what they would regret the following morning.

My love for Mexico persisted. Her *comida y canciones* (cuisine and songs) and the generous spirit of her inhabitants filled my heart. Often, I felt more at home in that country than in my own. Speaking Spanish fluently and longing for adventure, I had no fear of riding buses to visit small towns, the only *güera* (fair-haired female) aboard. Before the age of thirty, I had traveled alone throughout many parts of Mexico.

More often than not, I still ended up in simple kitchens, much to the surprise and delight of my humble hosts, who did not expect such enthusiasm for their country from a blonde *gringa*. And many times, that precious bottle of tequila, reserved for only very special occasions, was brought down from the shelf for a toast to friendship and to life.

In 1976, I visited La Perseverancia, the Sauza tequila distillery in the town of Tequila in Jalisco, Mexico. There I saw another lone blonde, dancing barefoot to her own tune, her scarlet sheath slipping from her shoulders. An expression of sheer pleasure lit her face. One hand was flung in the air, clutching a bottle of tequila; the other linked her to a circle of dark-haired Mexican maidens frolicking in Bacchanalian delight. This blonde's image hung on the thick-plastered walls of the distillery, part of a mural painted by Gabriel Flores, depicting the fateful discovery and production of tequila in the sixteenth century. I was astonished: the blonde in the painting even looked liked me! My curiosity was aroused. I knew I wanted to learn more about tequila, the seductive spirit that sang to my soul.

So began another Mexican journey, this time, a tequila quest. I visited fields planted with endless rows of *agaves*, formidable plants with a profusion of swordlike blades exploding from a central core. In rustic and modern distilleries alike, I watched the *agave*'s magical transformation into tequila, the spirit of Mexico. I tasted shimmering silver tequilas directly from copper-pot stills and golden-hued ones from fine oak casks. And I ate memorable meals in the homes of field workers as well as distillery owners.

As a cook, I recognized tequila's potential in the kitchen as well as in the cantina but was surprised to find that Mexicans seldom cooked with it. Tequila's versatile nature—lively, peppery, and robust with herbaceous and fruity characteristics—complemented my own style of cooking. I eagerly embarked upon a new culinary adventure, using recipes to showcase tequila in a festive way in food and drinks. With emphasis on garnish and presentation, I created drinks that highlight tequila in fresh and bright ways, taking tequila far beyond the ubiquitous margarita. In this celebratory fashion, one drink becomes a special event.

Today, beans and corn, chiles and chocolate remain highly acknowledged treasures of the New World. Yet the gift of the *agave* often remains overlooked. As the first distilled spirit of the Americas, tequila is richly imbued with history, heritage, and tradition. Even the mention of its name conjures up images of fun and fiesta.

Join me in stepping out of that circle of drunken revelry depicted in the distillery painting from long ago. Let's gather together, linking arms and raising glasses, as fellow tequila enthusiasts with a respect and reverence for the spirit that has withstood the test of time. Let's raise our glasses in appreciation, a toast to tequila, the national drink of Mexico. And, yes, upon the first sip, we hear the mariachis begin to play!

The author with friends, Mariachi Estrella. *Photo by Bill Records*

"La Sirena"
The Mermaid
Temptress...
hand carved
and painted
by Pedro Marcos
Guerrero,
Mexico

ABOUT TEQUILA, PULQUE, AND MEZCAL

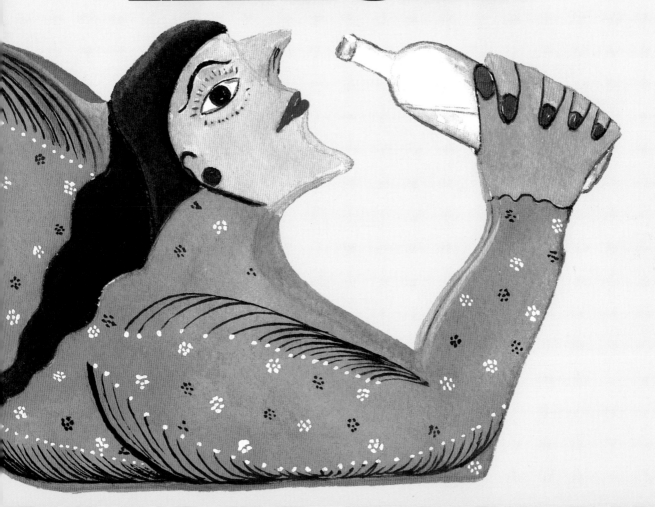

THE TRUTH ABOUT TEQUILA

El hombre que toma vino
es un hombre divino.
El que no lo toma,
es como una rosa sin aroma

A man who drinks tequila
is a most divine gent.
He who doesn't drink it,
is like a rose without scent.

In 1973, more than a million cases of tequila were sold in the United States. Tequila's south-of-the-border mystique evoked images of dust and bravado, barroom brawls, and the *"uno-dos-tres"* ritual: a lick of salt, a swig of fiery brew, and a bite into a juicy wedge of lime to remedy the aftertaste. Tequila became the belle of rowdy cantinas and fraternity fêtes, known primarily as the macho potion to imbibe in rapid succession as "shooters" chased with beer, or else camouflaged in sweet concoctions. Tequila had a reputation to overcome, a history to defend, and an image to change.

The past ten years may well be remembered as tequila's golden decade, an era of enlightenment. The margarita has become the number-one mixed drink of demand throughout much of the United States. Aficionados now call their shots and sip fine aged tequilas from snifters. Trend-setting tequilas line store shelves and the bars of upscale restaurants, fetching prices equal to those of V.S.O.P. Cognac. José Cuervo Tequila's annual sales alone rocketed to over 1.5 million cases in 1993.

Yet, despite its booming popularity, tequila remains the most misunderstood of spirits, its reputation tarnished by erroneous information regarding its origin, production, and characteristic effects.

"Copitas"
talavera shot glasses
Dolores Hidalgo,
Guanajuato

LA VERDAD
THE TRUTH

- Tequila is a fiesta! It makes you dance and sing with the the mariachis and each sip sends you south of the border (without leaving home).

- Tequila, shots, and margaritas are simply made for each other, and lime and salt are their natural accompaniments. But fine tequila may also be sipped and savored as one would a fine cognac or a single-malt Scotch.

- Tequila is a finely crafted spirit regulated by Mexican government standards similar to the French laws governing cognac. Tequila can taste as fine as V.S.O.P. Cognac or as bad as cheap brandy, depending on the manner in which it was produced.

  - Tequila never has a worm in the bottle, although *mezcal*, another agave distillate, traditionally does.

  - Tequila is not made from any cactus at all; instead, it is derived from the *agave*, a plant more akin to a lily than a cactus.

  - Tequila may make you see 400 rabbits if you drink too much, but it is not an hallucinogen.

  - Tequila comes in four styles: silver, gold, *reposado* (rested), and *añejo* (aged). These vary in style, quality, and price. There are many brands; taste them to find your own personal favorites!

"La Virgen de Guadalupe" the Patroness of the Americas with maguey...

colorfully painted ceramic Virgin of Guadalupe by Esteban Basilio Volasco Ocomicho, Michoacán

"El Diablo"
The Devil...
painted wooden
devil—
limbs move
when string is
pulled
Oaxaca,
Mexico

MENTIRAS
LIES

- Tequila makes you dance with the devil, puts snakes in your head, and sends you crawling home on your knees.

- Tequila tastes like firewater and must be guzzled rapidly in shots, camouflaged in margaritas, or accompanied by lime juice and salt to disguise its flavor.

- Tequila is Mexican moonshine.

- Tequila has a dead-drunk worm at the bottom of every bottle.

- Tequila is made from a cactus.

- Tequila comes from the peyote (*mescal*) cactus, just like the hallucinogenic drug mescaline (*mescalito*).

- Tequila comes in only one style and only one brand.

A GLOSSARY

AGAVE

Agave is the name of a genus of plants classified by Carolus Linnaeus, derived from the Greek word for "noble" or "admirable." Agaves were once classified either in the family *Amaryllidaceae* or *Liliaceae*, along with lilies, aloes, and amaryllis. Botanists today give the agave merit of its own, in the family *Agavaceae*. More than 120 species have been recorded in the Americas. Tequila, mezcal, and pulque are alcoholic beverages made from various species of the agave.

METL

Metl was the Náhuatl name given collectively to many species of agave. Early codices (chronicles of pre-Hispanic culture typically written on paper made from agave fiber), cited descriptions and virtues of fourteen species of agave.

MEZCAL

Mezcal is derived from the Náhuatl word *mexcalmetl*, meaning "agave species." In Mexico today, the term *mezcal* refers both to the agave and to the powerful distillate made from it.

MESCAL

Mescal is the English spelling for mezcal and the name for the peyote cactus (*Lophophora williamsii*), from which mescaline is produced. Mescal is also the name of the hallucinatory "bean" or seed of the mountain laurel (*Sophora secundiflora*). Neither the cactus nor the laurel is related to the agave.

MAGUEY

Maguey is the common name for the agave in Mexico. The Spanish explorers named it after a plant that they first encountered in the Caribbean. The word *maguey* is used interchangeably with *agave* or *mezcal*.

The Blue Agave

THE SPIRIT OF MEXICO:
From agave fields to cantina

Champaña, tinto, y jerez
es cóndanlos avergonzados,
o marchen precipitados
para su tierra otra vez.

☼

Claret, sherry, and champagne,
hide them all with shame,
or return to your homeland
as fast as you possibly can.

An understanding of the agave will give you a newfound reverence both for the plant itself and for its gift of tequila. Unlike grapes and grain, which can be harvested every year for making wine and spirits, an agave must grow for nearly a decade before it can be harvested. Once in its lifetime, the agave shoots a gigantic flowering spear into the sky, a brave warrior's final triumph, then dies. The agave most commonly recognized in the Southwestern United States is the century plant (*Agave americana*). Although many people mistakenly assume that it blooms only once in a century, in fact it blooms once in a decade.

The agave has flourished for thousands of years throughout semiarid regions of Mexico, where other plants wither during the ruthless seasons of drought. Born of ashes, a phoenix among plants, the agave appears to have erupted out of molten volcanic earth. Its swordlike arms reach for the heavens, each blade a tapered trough directing precious rainwater to its core, where it is hoarded for times when water is scarce. A prolific plant, the agave flourishes in the wild.

The Illustrious Agave
(La Milagrosa—The Miraculous One)

Agave is a gift from Mother Earth. Mexico's indigenous peoples cleverly discovered how to utilize every part of the plant for their daily survival, selecting the best attributes from its many species. It's no wonder that the agave had such mystical and sacred significance to the early Mexicans. They wasted nothing. They ate her flowers. They quenched their thirst by tapping her central core, savoring the *aguamiel* (honey-water) from within. They buried meat wrapped in her fresh leaves on hot coals to keep it succulent and flavorful while cooking. Even the worm that resided in the plant became a delicacy.

These native people also roasted the heart of the agave, which converted its starchy core into a sweet and nutritional food source. This sacrificial heart—for indeed the entire plant died upon its removal—offered vital sustenance far beyond that of the symbolic offering of human sacrifice.

But the magical agave provided more than nourishment. The people made needles and nails, ornaments and weapons from the spiky tip of the agave's large leaves. They extracted the coarse fiber from within the leaves and wove it into cloth, mats and baskets. And, from the protective cuticle within the agave's leaves, they produced a parchment-like paper, which they then used for writing upon and for wrapping steamed, seasoned meats.

Today, millions of maguey (the common name for agave) cover the Mexican landscape. They are commonly planted close together to form protective fences around property. For centuries, *campesinos* (country dwellers) have used these plants in ancestral ways. Almost everything they needed for a simple lifestyle was contained within one plant. Certain species produce sisal for sandals, henequen for rope, vinegar and sugar, medicine and soap. Even the dead leaves are employed as roofing for houses and fuel for fires.

Also of great significance, the admirable agave produces the three national drinks of Mexico: pulque, mezcal, and tequila. Great confusion surrounds this trio, and they are often mistaken for one and the same. But each is derived from a different species of agave, generally grown in different regions of Mexico. Although pulque, mezcal, and tequila are all members of the same *Agavaceae* family, they are cousins, not siblings, and have very different characteristics.

The production of mezcal and tequila requires field workers to uproot the entire agave plant in order to remove its starchy core. When baked, this core is converted into the fermentable sugars necessary for distillation. Pulque, on the other hand, has an entirely different means of production: its fermentable juices are tapped while the plant is still alive. Always served fresh, pulque is a naturally fermented drink that is never distilled.

The Blue Agave

Pulque

- Pulque (POOL-keh) is a milky-white, foamy, viscous beverage with a mildly intoxicating alcohol content of four to six percent. Pulque has been consumed in Mexico for more than two thousand years.

- Pulque is produced from fermenting the *aguamiel* (honey-water) tapped from within the heart of one of several species of large, succulent agaves (primarily *Agave atrovirens*, *A. salmiana*, and *A. mapisaga*) found in high, cool, semiarid regions of Mexico's Central Plateau (most notably in the states of Hidalgo, Mexico, and Puebla).

- Pulque is produced in *tinacales* (fermentation houses), where a potent and naturally occurring bacteria promotes rapid fermentation.

- Pulque is a regional drink because it is highly perishable and does not transport easily. It cannot be canned or bottled.

- Pulque may be "cured" (flavored) with one or more of the following to make it more palatable: fruits and vegetables, nuts and grains, herbs and chiles, sugar and spice, eggs, and cream.

- Pulque is rich in nutrients, protein, amino acids, mineral salts, sugars, and vitamins B, C, D, and E. It has long been known for its nutritive attributes and is renowned as a medicine, a restorative, and an alleged aphrodisiac.

- Pulque was once the divine drink of Aztec nobility, Spanish conquistadors, Independence revolutionaries, bohemian artists, and landed gentry.

- Pulque today is generally regarded as the drink of Mexico's lower class because it is very inexpensive. Pulque, unfortunately, is rapidly being replaced by beer and cheap grain alcohol.

- Pulque is never distilled into tequila.

THE FIRST DRINKING BINGE

In order to prevent public drunkenness and dissention, Aztec rulers imposed strict laws governing the consumption of pulque: offenders were sometimes clubbed or strangled to death! By way of compensation, however, the five "dead days" at the end of the Aztec calendar year were set aside for ritualized public intoxication. Participants communally slurped pulque through reed straws from a stone vessel, which was continually refilled with the frothy brew. During the remaining 360 days of the year, pulque was reserved for the aged and the infirm, nobles, warriors, and nursing mothers.

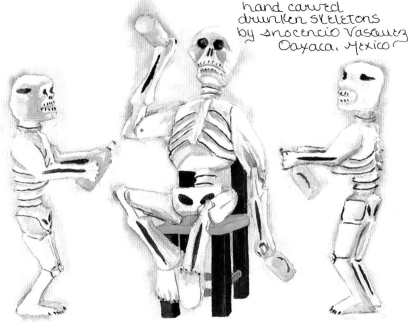

hand carved drunken skeletons by Inocencio Vasquez Oaxaca, Mexico

In Search of Pulque

To better understand tequila's virtues, I decided to learn more about pulque, the original agave inebriant. I flew to Mexico City and from there drove with a guide two hours northward into the state of Hidalgo. We passed Teotihuacán and the magical pyramids of the sun and moon—now ruins, mere reminders of lost gods.

Spiny *nopal* (prickly pear) cactus and giant maguey covered the roadside, patches of green in a sun-baked land. The magueys' huge spiky *pencas* (leaves) spiraled from their centers, bending gracefully with open arms, some of them tattooed with the carved initials of lovers.

These agaves of Mexico's Central Plateau are of a much larger species than those that thrive in the hotter and drier tequila-producing regions of Mexico. Many are over six feet tall and just as wide; their large, fleshy gray-green leaves bear little resemblance to the narrow, silvery sword-like blades of those agaves used to make tequila.

As we approached Apan, once the heart of Mexico's pulque-producing region, I was surprised to see so few magueys. Instead, a dust bowl of parched, eroded earth and dried corn greeted us. Pulque, I would learn, was not easy to find. Huge haciendas resembling feudal castles loomed on the horizon; today they produce fighting bulls instead of the pulque for which they once were acclaimed.

My guide and I drove down a desolate dirt road just outside of San Juan Ixtilmaco, sharing it with a herd of rowdy goats. Eventually we arrived at a crumbling adobe hut, its windows boarded up with metal scraps to keep out the dust. Mario Gómez Amador, a humble farmer and *pulquero* (one who makes pulque), tipped his straw sombrero to welcome us. We asked for pulque and he went inside, returning with a blue plastic pail filled with a milky-white, frothy liquid.

Scooping a *jícaro* (a gourd serving as a bowl and ladle) into the pail, he topped it with some creamy white foam, and handed it to me. I certainly had second thoughts as I raised it to my lips, gulping it down and nearly gagging on the albuminous consistency. Nevertheless, I found its flavor intriguing: slightly sweet yet acrid, yeasty, earthy, and herbaceous, with a hint of salt.

At once I understood the ancients' reverence for this mystical drink. Just as the hermaphroditic characteristics of the maguey suggest both phallus (stalk) and lactiferous breast (*aguamiel*), pulque embodies the essence of man and woman. Simultaneously it is reminiscent of mother's milk and semen. For obvious reasons, the ancients greatly revered this clearly symbolic gift from the gods.

Señor Amador took me to a field where a few precious agave plants grew amid stalks of corn. I asked him why there were so few. He replied that pulque had lost its demand. Instead of raising maguey, wealthy landowners now raise cattle, overgrazing the land and not replenishing it with agave. *"Por eso no tenemos lluvia. El maguey llama la lluvia. Ahora hay poco maguey, poca lluvia,"* he said sadly as he looked toward the heavens. (This is the reason we have no rain. The maguey call forth the rain. Now we have few maguey, little rain.) Still, he patiently waits for his maguey to mature.

He explained that when the plant is from eight to twelve years old, its *corazón* (heart, or center core from which its new leaves continually unfold) elongates, preparing itself for its mighty thrust toward the sky. At this crucial time, the emerging stalk must be "castrated" so that the maguey's vital juices will be contained within the plant instead of used to feed the flowering stalk.

Agua de las verdes matas,
tú me tumbas,
tú me matas,
tú me haces andar a gatas.

✺

Nectar of the green maguey,
you knock me down,
you knock me out,
you make me reel and sway.

"Chupando el Aguamiel
con el Acocote"
Syphoning the honey water
with a gourd
molded and painted clay scene
Jalisco,
Mexico

Leche de la Vaca Verde
(Milk from the Green Cow)

Within a few months, when the castration scar heals, Senor Amador begins to extract the aguamiel stored within the central core. He removes a large stone from the center of the plant (placed there to keep out thirsty animals in the night), disclosing a hollow cavity filled with a clear liquid. Legend says that pulque was discovered when a farmer's wife observed a mouse gnawing a hole in the heart of the maguey from which to drink the naturally fermenting aguamiel within.

Still employing the pre-Hispanic techniques of his ancestors, Señor Amador dips the narrow end of a long-necked *acocote* into the cavity "*para chupar el aguamiel*" (to siphon the sweet sap) from within. It tastes fresh, pure, and soothing—with nuances of herb-scented honey and desert rain. At this stage, the aguamiel is highly nutritive and has medicinal value—and purported powers as an aphrodisiac.

Then, like his fellow *tlachiqueros* (from the Náhuatl word meaning "those who scrape"), Señor Amador scrapes away some of the fibrous pulp from within the now-empty cavity. Scraping with a *raspador*, a short-handled tool whose blade resembles a large metal fingernail, he enlarges the cavity, at the same time encouraging more aguamiel to flow.

At dawn and dusk he repeats this ritual of his forefathers, collecting about half a gallon of the precious honey-water daily. This process also prevents fermentation from occurring naturally within the plant. Within six months, the plant perishes, a vegetal spring run dry.

Pulqueros take the aguamiel that they collect from the fields in barrels to *tinacales*, or fermentation houses. During the height of pulque production in the nineteenth century, pulque provided great tax revenues for Mexico and pulque haciendas flourished. Now, tinacales are scarce. Those that do exist welcome neither strangers nor women. The art of the tinacal remains secretive and sacred with knowledge passed down for generations. Sadly, like so many ancient customs in Mexico, the magic and the mastery, the ritual and the tradition of the tinacal is becoming a thing of the past.

Today, aguamiel is fermented in oak barrels instead of the traditional cowhide troughs; little else is required. A naturally occurring and very potent bacteria *Termobacterium mobile* (sometimes augmented with oak leaves and herbs) causes fermentation. This process takes about a week, at which point the aguamiel changes from a clear and still liquid to a frothy, white, and mildly alcoholic beverage, and it must be transported as soon as possible to where it will be consumed.

Because pulque is not distilled, it is highly perishable and sours rapidly, changing from pleasant to putrid (with an ammonia-like odor) within days, especially when not stored well. The Náhuatl name for pulque at this "sour" stage was *octli poliuhqui*, from which the word *pulque* may have derived. Unfortunately, today good fresh pulque is difficult to find; many people have tasted only that which lives up to its rank reputation. Most people will never taste fresh pulque, the *cara blanca*, the pure white milk of Mayahuel, ancient goddess of the maguey.

Blanco bueno
y puro
Sólo en el tinacal
lo jura.

Pulque white
and pure
only in the tinacal
for sure.

Pulquerías: Mexico's first cantinas

Pulquerías (pulque bars), like the tinacales, are rapidly disappearing in Mexico. They flourished during the mid nineteenth and early twentieth centuries, when this "most Mexican of drinks" exemplified the national spirit of Mexico. Pulquerías had brightly painted façades and picturesque names. Typically the names had double meanings or were peppered with humor that was grim, or bawdy, or tongue-in-cheek: A Trip to the Moon, Blood of the Maguey, The Great Wound, Memories of the Future, and My Life as Another are a few examples.

Inside, the walls were painted with imaginative murals, and colorful paper banners welcomed those who entered: artists and writers, politicians and landed gentry, and many less illustrious folk. Humor and wit flowed as freely as the pulque, which was poured into a variety of mugs and pitchers. These were given a wide variety of names, some according to the amounts they held, some after women, and some with off-color double meaning nicknames like Cabrón (Old Goat) or Tornillo (because of the corkscrew shape of the glass).

Today, sawdust floors reeking of spilled pulque and the despair of the lower class are too often all that remains of a proud national tradition. Mexican law once prohibited women, men in uniform, and dogs from entering pulquerías. In 1981, the law was overturned, allowing women to enter, but dogs and uniformed men are still not allowed! Most women, however, still prefer to obtain their glasses of pulque by stretching their arms through a small window from a cubicle outside the pulquería. I went a step farther, of course, and stepped inside.

La Pirata in Mexico City was as busy and rowdy as any bar at happy hour, except that it was eleven o' clock in the morning and only men were inside! Many of them appeared to have been drinking all night. (I still cannot understand how anyone could consume enough of the mildly alcoholic and bloating brew to become intoxicated.) Others were simply in for a morning perk-up (pulque is much more nutritious than coffee), gossip and camaraderie. Some of the men played dominoes, others sang along with a tattered trio of musicians. And some had simply laid their heads down upon the table.

An altar to La Virgen de Guadalupe hung on the wall, as it does in almost every pulquería. A gigantic stone molcajete piled high with guacamole sat on the counter, compliments of the house. It was heavily garnished with chopped onions and long sprigs of cilantro, resembling some strange vegetative headdress. Although I was forewarned of its fire, I scooped some of it onto a warm tortilla and took a big bite. Immediately, an explosion of serrano peppers assaulted my tongue (a good way to sell more pulque, no doubt), and the room broke out in good-natured laughter.

A motley assortment of glasses, gourds, pitchers, mugs, and a vat of foamy white pulque lined the back of the bar. The barrel-chested bartender, Salvador Navarrete, enthusiastically took my order, humorously scorning any man daring to pay me attention. Many of the men were drinking from liter mugs, but I chose a small glass. The pulque was fresh and smooth. I couldn't imagine that it had alcoholic effects; it seemed surprisingly nutritious instead.

The bartender also ladled pastel-colored *curados* (flavored pulques resembling "smoothies") from large aluminum pots that were painted with cheerful fruits and had a block of ice inside to keep the contents cool. I sampled these and they were quite delicious. My favorites were those made from tart fruits such as lime (with some of the peel), guava, prickly pear, and pineapple. One flavored with celery and alfalfa tasted as if it had miraculous curative properties, while the one thickened with egg yolk and almonds and dusted with cinnamon tasted like a sumptuous dessert. I did not, however, brave the raw oyster plopped in a glass of pulque topped with *salsa picante* and a squeeze of fresh lime. These original "oyster shooters" have fabled powers as an aphrodisiac.

I can't say that I recommend pulquerías for those unaccustomed to the language and customs of Mexico. Unfortunately, many of the pulquerías accessible to tourists serve artificially flavored pulques, just as many bars today serve artificially flavored margaritas. The more traditional pulquerías may not welcome strangers, and one must also take caution not to drink pulque that has been adulterated with unpurified ice or water.

Many Mexicans believe that pulque continues to ferment in the stomach once ingested and that a shot of mezcal is essential *"para despanzar"* (to ease bloating). Sounds to me like a good excuse to drink more, and a stronger spirit at that!

Si tomas para olvidar,
paga antes de tomar.

❋

If you drink to forget,
pay first.

MAYAHUEL, GODDESS OF FOUR HUNDRED BREASTS

Mayahuel was the Aztec goddess of motherhood and moonlight and of the pure white pulque that flowed from one of her four hundred breasts. This she reserved for her favorite son, Ome Tochtli. He was symbolized as a *conejo* (rabbit) and, along with four hundred other rabbit dieties, he reigned over the four hundred different kinds of drinks made from pulque (see *curados* above) and the four hundred consequences of drinking them. Apparently, four hundred was the magical number for infinite possibilities (or the number of rabbits seen hopping through one's head when in a state of inebriation).

Mezcal

- Mezcal (mess-KAHL) is a clear and potent high-proof distillate.

- Mezcal is derived from one of several species of agave, primarily *Agave angustifolia*, which is grown in the warmer and lower semiarid regions of Mexico than those in which the pulque-producing agaves flourish.

- Mezcal is commonly produced by the traditional handcrafted method, often in remote and rustic stills without government regulation.

- Mezcal is a regional drink mainly consumed and bottled in its place of origin. Because of the small quantity of agave and lack of quality control, it is not widely exported.

- Mezcal has a characteristic smoky flavor and is commonly sweetened and flavored with fruits, herbs, and nuts to make it more palatable.

- Mezcal is regarded by many Mexicans as a tonic, a digestif, a diuretic, and an aphrodisiac.

- Mezcal is consumed throughout much of Mexico and is typically known by regional names.

- Mezcal often has a worm in the bottle.

Brightly painted ceramic "gusano"

from Santa Cruz de las Huertas, Jalisco

WHY IS THERE A WORM IN THE BOTTLE?

Chinicuiles, small red worms (actually moth larvae of *Comadia redtenbachi*) also known as *gusanos rojos*, live in the roots of the maguey. They are toasted on a hot *comal* (griddle), giving them a pungent, nutty flavor. Small packets of *sal de gusano* are sometimes tied around the necks of bottles of mezcal, both for their unique flavor and as a sales gimmick. *Meocoiles* (larvae of *Aegiale hesperarius*), also known as *gusanos blancos* live inside the leaves and are considered a delicacy. Either *gusano* may also be found floating around the bottom of a bottle of mezcal.

According to *Náhuatl* legend, the gusano, having once lived within the maguey, ingested the magical spirit of that plant. Some still believe that the gusano gives the mezcal a spirit of its own. He who swallows the worm in the bottle ingests the soul of the maguey. That seemingly lowly worm:

▼ Adds flavor to the mezcal with its inherent protein and fats

▼ Verifies that the mezcal is an agave distillate because the gusano lives in the agave plant

▼ Honors the lucky guest who gets to swallow it (Professional biologist and tequila aficionada Donna Howell says, "Considering that the worm isn't offered until the bottle is drained down to its level, one seldom minds.")

▼ Makes a marvelous sales gimmick: almost everyone has heard about the worm in the bottle. Besides, if you bite into the worm, you will surely need another sip!

In Search of Mezcal

On the streets surrounding Oaxaca's bustling Mercado Benito Juárez, small shops sell local specialties: cinnamon-laced chocolate, burnished black pottery, and multi-hued textiles handwoven on back-strap looms. Brightly colored façades (resembling those of the early pulquerías) lure potential customers, especially tourists, into mezcal dispensaries.

Inside, shelves lined with a colorful selection of mezcals promise delight to souvenir seekers. Handpainted bottles, black pottery *ollas* (crocks), painted earthenware monkeys in straw hats, and pigskin flasks await purchase. Green-glazed shot glasses and whimsical *zapatillos*, shaped like a woman's leg (as well as more erotically suggestive containers hidden on bottom shelves) further the ambiance of these picturesque *tiendas* (stores).

Si tomas bastante mezcal,
puedes ver toda la mujer.

If you drink enough mezcal
you'll see the whole woman.

Small *jícaros* (gourd bowls) from which to sip mezcal, painted red and gaily adorned with flowers, are for sale along with small bags filled with salt. But this salt is most peculiar! Flavored with dried ground *gusanos* (worms that feast on the agave plant) and *pasilla* chiles, it ritually accompanies shots of mezcal, just as unflavored salt accompanies shots of tequila. Stacks of plastic jugs stand ready to be filled with mezcal directly from a large barrel. After all, in many Oaxacan homes, a bottle of mezcal is as likely a staple as a bag of *frijoles negros*. Many Mexicanos swear by a shot of mezcal at midmorning and one (at least) again before bed.

I sampled many kinds of mezcal, some quite remarkable and complex: characteristically smoky and earthy with peppery overtones. Others tasted exceedingly crude—like a combination of charcoal fluid and lighter fluid burning all the way down my throat!

Like pulque, mezcal is often sweetened and flavored with fresh tropical fruits, citrus, herbs, or almonds (undoubtedly to mask its unrefined flavor). These flavored concoctions are temptingly called *cremas de mezcal*. One such fruit-flavored mezcal known as *pechuga almendrado* is also flavored with an uncooked chicken breast during distillation. This gives it a surprisingly rich flavor and pale amber color, which many Mexicans regard highly. Indeed, it tasted quite delicious—smooth and subtle. A cure-all swig from *mezcal poleo*, heady with the strong minty aroma of pennyroyal, was guaranteed to heal anything that ailed me (and was an aphrodisiac as well, I was told)!

Perhaps the mezcal most familiar to North Americans is *mezcal de gusanitos*, the one with the worm in the bottle. The unsuspecting worm resides in the maguey plant before being plopped into the bottle as proof of the proof! If the worm is truly pickled, the alcohol has not been diluted.

Upon returning from Oaxaca, I had a *Día de los Muertos* (Day of the Dead) fiesta at my home. Friends brought small tokens of remembrance of their deceased loved ones, and we made a memorial altar in a room filled with candlelight and flowers. I had brought back a bottle of pechuga almendrado

"EL Trio"
mezcal,
sal de gusano,
jícaro

The Trio
mezcal,
ground
worm salt,
drinking
gourd...

Mezcal

Gusanitos

Sal de Gusanos

hand painted
mezcal bottle
and gourd,
Oaxaca,
Mexico

and sal de gusano from Oaxaca. Guests drank the mezcal with gusto, many of them bravely accompanying it with a lick of the spicy salt sprinkled on their palms. Perhaps too many shots later, I passed around another Oaxacan specialty: small, fried *chapulines* (grasshoppers) spiced with lime and chile. "Trick or treat?" some wondered. Actually, they make a tasty, crunchy accompaniment for shots of mezcal.

Los chapulines:
si los comes,
vuelves a Oaxaca.
Mezcales:
si los tomes,
vuelves a Oaxaca.

❋

Grasshoppers:
if you eat them,
you will return to Oaxaca.
Mezcal:
if you drink it,
you will return to Oaxaca.

Oaxaqueños often travel to remote *palenques* (rustic shacks) outside Oaxaca City on the way to Mitla—to Matatlán, Tlacolula, and other hilly environs—with their plastic gallon jugs (or barrels) to fill with *mezcal de olla* produced by traditional means. Mezcal, the medicine: diuretic, digestif, restorer of spirits, cure for colds. Mezcal, the macho potion: lusty elixir, lover's panacea. Mezcal, Mexico's moonshine: distilled over charcoal fires in primitive stills.

Each cantina and mezcal shop in Oaxaca seems to have its own private stock of mezcal collected from some family member's still in a remote area. Some of the best mezcal I tasted was crudely presented in a bottle with no label (it had previously contained soda pop). Some large and commercial distilleries exist, but for the most part, quality control and quantity of mature agave are lacking. Exportation of mezcal remains limited.

I observed mezcal being made in Oaxaca much in the same manner as it was made by the early Spaniards. The *espadín*, the preferred maguey for making Oaxacan mezcal, takes about eight years to mature, at which time field workers remove the starchy central cores from the plant. These cores are cut in half and steamed over hot coals in underground stone-lined pits covered with maguey leaves and damp earth. This method gives the mezcal its unique smoky flavor and also converts the starch into a very sweet and fibrous pulp. A mule pulled a large, heavy stone wheel called a *tahona* in a circle, crushing the pulp to extract the sweet fermentable juices that would be distilled after fermenting in tanks for four to five days.

The flavor of mezcal varies tremendously, depending upon the variety of maguey and the production methods used. Some distillers use copper pot stills and oak fermenting tanks, while others use crude metal equipment. Because mezcal is traditionally distilled only once, impurities remain. At best, it can have a complex and engaging flavor; at worst, it can taste harsh and unrefined. Some mezcal is sweetened and/or flavored during distillation, and some is reposed for a few years in oak, but most mezcal is consumed directly after distillation.

Because of tequila's booming popularity, I believe mezcal will soon be in the spotlight as well and will become more widely available. In fact, I have heard that Oaxaca is attempting to establish laws that will regulate mezcal's production, setting standards of quality similar to those that regulate tequila.

Thus far, however, I find that the mezcal imported into the United States lacks soul. In an attempt to imitate its cousin, tequila, modern production methods (including a second distillation) have subdued mezcal's distinctive personality. Its characteristic smoke-and-fire flavor is missing in most imported brands. It tastes nothing like the mezcal I savored in Oaxaca—the mystical land of the Mixtec and Zapotec.

Aficionados of traditionally made mezcal sing its praises as a pure and natural agave distillate. They claim it is made from 100-percent agave without the sugars and flavorings sometimes added by commercial tequila producers.

Tequileros (tequila producers) disagree. They espouse tequila's virtues as a smoother and more sophisticated spirit carefully regulated by law to assure its quality and integrity. Tequila always undergoes a second distillation, which removes impurities and undesirable alcohols, leaving a more refined spirit.

But perhaps most important, tequileros believe that the various agaves used for making mezcal simply lack the inherent sweetness and flavor of the agave from which tequila is made. Whereas mezcal can be made from several types of agave (some with soapy or bitter characteristics), tequila can be made from only one: the *blue* agave. This, they say, is what makes tequila so special and inimitable.

When the Spaniards colonized Mexico, they soon longed for a spirit more potent and palatable than pulque, one more akin to the brandy of their homeland. These enterprising Iberians discovered that the ubiquitous maguey held more promise than just pulque; roasting the heart of these plants yielded the fermentable sugars necessary for distillation. Using copper pot stills they had brought with them from the Old World and ancient, Moorish distillation methods, they produced the first distilled spirit of the Americas: *vino de mezcal*. Its 110 proof made pulque indeed seem like mother's milk.

Mezcal can be distilled from one of several species of maguey grown in semiarid regions of Mexico. These *magueyes mescaleros* (mezcal-producing magueys) thrive in lower and warmer regions than the *magueyes pulqueros* (pulque-producing magueys). The mezcal best known to North Americans is that which comes from the state of Oaxaca. Mezcal, however, is also produced throughout the heart of the Mexican plains (including the tequila-producing states) into the Chihuahuan desert, along a wide stretch of the Pacific coast and into the southern state of Chiapas.

Typically, mezcal is known by regional names. For instance, *sotol*, from the Chihuahuan desert, is made from agaves in the genus *Dasyliron*, while *bacanora*, named after the area in Sonora from which it is made, is derived from the *Agave angustifolia*. Few people realize that tequila, made from the *Agave tequilana*, is actually a regional variant of mezcal. In a *Texas Monthly* article, Gregory Curtis explained, "Tequila is mezcal, but not all mezcal is tequila," just like all cognac is brandy but not all brandy is cognac. Mexican law governs tequila's production, distinguishing it from other mezcals to guarantee its unique flavor and characteristics.

Tequila

- Tequila (teh-KEE-luh), unlike pulque and mezcal, is regulated by Mexican law, NORMA, which sets standards of quality.

- Tequila is a high-proof regional agave distillate. It is clear and colorless upon distillation but may be aged in oak for added flavor and color.

- Tequila is made only from one species of agave, the *Agave tequilana* Weber, "blue" variety, whose silvery-blue leaves and characteristic flavor distinguish it from other agaves.

- Tequila is produced only from agaves grown in five Mexican states: the entire state of Jalisco, and designated areas in Guanajuato, Michoacan, Nayarít, and Tamaulipas.

- Tequila is made from the distillation of fermented agave juice. NORMA requires that 51 percent of the fermentable sugars must come from the "blue" agave; the remaining 49 percent may come from additional sugars.

- Tequila is sold in four categories, per NORMA: *tequila añejo* (aged), *tequila blanco* (white, or "silver"), *tequila joven abocado* (gold), and *tequila reposado* (reposed).

- Tequila can be made exclusively of 100 percent *Agave tequilana* Weber, "blue" variety, (with no added sugars) but must say so on the label and must be bottled in Mexico.

- Tequila is one of the fastest growing spirits in the industry, with 4.5 million cases sold in 1993. The United States consumes nearly 90 percent of exported tequila.

Papier Mâche
Day of the Dead
Skeleton
Mexico City

NORMA OFICIAL MEXICANA (NOM)

On March 31, 1978, NORMA Oficial Mexicana (NOM-V-7-1978) was established to set standards of quality in the production of tequila, much as the French Apellation Contrôllé set standards of quality in the production of cognac. The Mexican government established these laws to distinguish tequila from other mezcals and to help tequila producers meet government requirements for the production of tequila.

The letters **NOM** (or **DGN** on labels prior to 1978), followed by four numbers and the letter **I,** are designated on every bottle to show that the tequila within complies with the established norms. NORMA establishes the characteristics necessary for an agave distillate to be called tequila (see the list on page 27-28).

The Lily of the Field
(Blue Agave)

Over eight hundred million acres of blue agave grow in the state of Jalisco alone. In such profusion, they appear as an unexpected sea of silver, contrasting with the rugged earthiness of the Mexican plains. This variety of agave is known as "blue" for the silvery blue color of its long, stiff leaves, each one tipped with a piercing thorn, its edges lined with a tidy row of small but menacing ridges. The swordlike armor of the agave harbors a hidden treasure. Buried deep within these protective arms lies a heart of gold—a starchy core which can be converted into fermentable sugars.

This highly esteemed "blue" variety, the *Agave tequilana* Weber, is the only agave from which tequila can be made. It is not a cactus, but more closely akin to a lily, and flourishes in an arid climate in volcanic soil, which is rich in minerals, ash, and silicate (the word *tequila* is, in fact, derived from the Náhuatl word for volcano). Ideal growing conditions, coupled with the inherent qualities of this particular agave, ultimately give tequila its characteristic flavor. If grown in other environments, the flavor of the agave is simply not of the same quality. Similarly, cognac can be made only from grapes grown within a delimited region of France. To protect the integrity of tequila, in 1978 the Mexican government established laws called NORMA (see page 20) to govern the production of tequila, much as the French Appellation Contrôllée governs the production of cognac. NORMA set quality standards and controls and designated specific regions of origin for the blue agave: most notably, the entire state of Jalisco, parts of the neighboring states of Nayarit, Michoacán, and Guanajuato, and areas within the eastern state of Tamaulipas.

However, most tequila is produced in two areas of Jalisco, where some thirty-six distilleries may be found today. The dry, volcanic soil of the Sierra Madre foothills (about thirty-five miles northwest of Guadalajara) is home to tequila's largest producers. Tequila has been made in this region since the seventeenth century and its production is highly mechanized. Here, in the small town of Tequila, José Cuervo and Sauza, tequila's founding families, produce their product in unassuming distilleries behind thick plaster walls. The most modern sight in this dusty town is the glistening stainless-steel tanker trucks filled with tequila bound for bottling in the United States. Nearby, in the even smaller town of Amatitán, Herradura tequila is distilled on a family estate.

Directly across the state lies the high plateau of the *Los Altos* region. Extending sixty miles northeast of Guadalajara, this rich agricultural area is noted for its red iron-oxide soil and robust agaves. Due, in part, to poor roads (even today they sometimes become impassable during the rainy season) this region is better known for its smaller distilleries and traditional, handcrafted methods of production, similar to the way Oaxacan mezcal is made. Many of these producers have only recently begun implementing commercial methods. The tequilas produced in this area include El Tesoro, Patrón, El Viejito, Porfidio, and Centinela.

In 1989, I was fortunate enough to join Tom Snell, Cuervo's vice-president of U.S. sales, when he led a tour to *La Rojeña*, the Cuervo distillery in Tequila. Tom enthusiastically shared his vast knowledge about tequila and his deep love for the people and culture of Mexico. We drove from Guadalajara, down the two-lane highway linking Mexico City with the Pacific coast. Fortunately, a profusion of golden sunflowers, dried corn, and miles of intriguing hand-stacked stone walls marking parcels of land kept my attention from the high-speed chase of diesels and dilapidated pickups constantly swerving around our bus. Within half an hour, we seemed to have stepped back in time. Guadalajara, Mexico's second largest city, seemed far away. The majestic Sierra Madre loomed on the horizon, and an extinct volcano lay straight ahead. Small stands on the sides of the road sold cowhide flasks filled with tequila, and agave was everywhere.

The bus stopped at one of Cuervo's agave fields, where many on the tour soon realized for the first time that tequila is not derived from a lowly cactus growing in the wild. On the contrary, the blue agave requires years of maintenance and care in order to develop optimum flavor. Patience is a virtue in the land of *mañana*, especially when it comes to the growing of agave: these plants take from eight to twelve years to mature! At this point, their ripened central cores are ready for harvesting.

A machine cannot determine the agave's maturity. Mature agaves are hand-selected for premium tequilas, just as only vine-ripened clusters of grapes are hand-chosen for vintage wine. Grapes, however, ripen in three months and the vine continues to produce for many years. The agave, on the other hand, bears its fruit but once in a lifetime. There can be no mistakes! Immature agaves will yield inadequate flavor and sugar content for producing quality tequila. And overripe agaves will rot in the field, a decade of waste.

The endless rows of agave, their thick, tough, spike-tipped leaves spiraling menacingly from a central core, prevent mechanization in the field. Beasts of burden can maneuver in the fields far more easily than heavy equipment. Most of the labor is done by hand by *mescaleros* whose precise and practiced harvesting techniques have been passed down for generations.

The harvest of the agave is continuous and depends upon the maturity of each agave plant. Approximately six months before its harvest, the mescaleros "castrate" the agave's emerging quiote (flowering stalk) which concentrates the plant's natural sugars in its core (sometimes they carve the date in one of the leaves as a reminder). Otherwise, the stalk would shoot ten feet into the sky, producing clusters of yellow flowers, seed pods, and baby plants simultaneously from its lofty nursery in the sky.

The Heart of the Matter: *La Jima*

José Fernandez Esparza, a silver-haired fifth-generation *mescalero* and field supervisor for Cuervo's vast estates, took us into a field full of mature agaves—some of them nearly six feet high. He pointed out the rather engorged base of one plant, whose leaves were beginning to wither slightly. This blue agave had reached its prime: the ceremony of *la jima* (the harvest) could begin.

The tools of the trade are simple: a machete, a shovel, and a *coa* (a flat, sharp-edged tool attached to a long wooden handle). Other necessities are sometimes tied around the *mescalero's* waist with a rope: a *triángulo* (file) used to sharpen the tools, and a cow's horn filled with lard to keep the hands from blistering.

Using a machete, a *jimador* (agave harvester) first whacked away some of the tough, spiky leaves radiating from the agave's central core. Then he severed its shallow roots with his *coa* and rolled the plant over on one side. Placing a foot upon the plant, he "rounded out" the heart of the agave, turning it as he shaved away the remaining leaves with swift and accurate strokes. Amazingly, what was left resembled a huge pineapple and is named *piña* after that same fruit. This process reminds me of plucking away the outer leaves of an artichoke in order to reach its delectable heart.

In less than three minutes the plant was harvested. With deft hands and the skilled artistry passed down for generations, one *jimador* may harvest one hundred plants a day! I will not even describe my clumsy attempts at harvesting. Suffice it to say that the piña was mutilated and I almost lost a foot.

A mature piña generally weighs from fifty to one hundred pounds. When sliced, it resembles a jícama inside: crisp and juicy, starchy and white. Although it has little flavor at this point, it is quite caustic; contact with skin will cause burning blisters and irritation, to which I can attest.

Workers strap about six of the piñas onto burros in the field to take them to trucks which carry them to the distillery, where fifteen pounds of piña will yield only one liter of tequila. Both in the fields and in the distilleries, workers carry the heavy piñas balanced upon their heads.

Approximately 2,000 blue agaves are planted per acre in Jalisco. The quality of the agave may vary, depending on the region in which it was grown and the care given to it in the fields—whether the agaves are grown in crowded rows or given ample space (six feet per plant). Each producer has their own standards: some use only estate-grown agaves, others purchase from a variety of growers. Throughout the agave's near-decade (or more!) of growth, it requires year-round care and mainte-nance, including: pruning the plant during June and July to encourage the piña's growth, weeding, fertilizing, insect and fungus control, optional drip irrigation and field maintenance, castrating the emerging quiote, harvesting the piñas, and transporting them to the distillery. During the rainy season (February–September), the *hijuelos* (young plants which emerge at the base of the "mother" plant during the fourth year of growth) are transplanted to other fields for propagation. ¡*La cosecha de agave que nunca se acabe!* (The wonderful agave crop, may it never, never stop!)

Las Piñas
Piñas strapped
on mule

"El Jimador"
The Agave
Harvester

Alchemy of a Magical Elixir

Once the piñas are unloaded in the *patios* of the distilleries, the magical alchemy of tequila begins. Each distillery has its unique methods of production, but whether produced in a rustic factory using traditional techniques or in a modern distillery with state-of-the-art equipment, the piñas must be baked to convert their inherent starch into the fermentable sugars.

Some distilleries use traditional stone and adobe *hornos* (ovens), in which the piñas are leisurely steamed, filling the distillery with a sweet and heady aroma. High-volume producers favor stainless steel autoclaves, which rapidly cook the piñas under pressure. Once cooked, the transformation is remarkable. Out of the ovens come large, fibrous chunks of caramel-colored agave (an edible delicacy), which resemble cooked sweet potatoes drenched in honey both in flavor and appearance.

Whether ground by a large stone *tahona* (grinding wheel) pulled by a mule or tractor, or by elaborate machines, the cooked agave is then shredded and washed with water to release all of its sugars. In traditional distilleries such as La Alteña, El Tesoro's distillery, a barefoot man carries this *mosto* (fermentable juices) on his head in heavy oak tubs to 1,500-liter wooden fermentation tanks, where it is mixed by hand. Modern distilleries pump it to huge stainless steel tanks holding as much as 20,000 liters. Fermentation may be gradual (up to six days), using naturally occurring yeasts and bacteria, or may be hurried with commercial yeasts and added sugars. While the yeasts and bacteria are alive and feasting on the sugars, the vats are filled with a warm, murky, bubbly brown liquid that is somewhat beer-like in flavor. By the final day of fermentation, the liquid is still and cool, and the sugars have converted into a mild alcohol.

Distillation may occur in traditional copper pot stills or in large stainless steel ones. During distillation, the fermented brew is heated to boiling. The resulting vapor is then condensed in a cooled coil, separating the alcohols and the impurities. By law, tequila must be distilled twice. The first distillation, called *ordinario*, produces a 38–40-proof distillate comprised of three strengths: *cabeza* (head), *cola* (tail), and *corazón* (heart), of which only the "heart" is saved. The heads and tails contain high and low alcohols, fusel oils, ethanol, and other impurities, which can give a harsh flavor and even be potentially toxic. The second (110-proof) distillation, usually followed by a filtering process, is essential for removing all impurities and giving tequila its characteristic flavor and clear color. Each distillery has its own "house style" of production, which accounts for the range of taste, quality, and price.

"La Piña"
The Heart
of the Agave

Four Categories of Tequila
Established by Mexican Law (NORMA)

Tequila is a versatile spirit. It varies in distinct styles from the fresh and clear agave distillate to that of golden hue, which has been aged in oak for several years. Quality, flavor, and price vary within these styles as well as among distilleries. Find the tequila styles (and distilleries) that best suit your personal taste. Be adventurous!

Tequila Blanco: White or Silver (Plata) Tequila

Mexican legal definition: *Tequila fresh from the still which may be brought to commercial proof with the addition of demineralized water.*

Silver tequilas are crystal clear and not influenced by wood or aging, although some producers allow their tequila to "rest" in wood or stainless steel tanks for up to forty-five days before bottling. Often the quality of the silver tequila will determine the style of the distillery.

Silver tequilas taste surprisingly smooth yet spirited, vibrant, herbaceous, and pleasantly peppery. I am a great fan of 100% agave silver tequilas which retain the discernible and natural sweetness of the agave often missing in aged spirits. Some silver tequila may taste fiery and feral with an unmistakable petrol finish! Unfortunately, these throat-searing tequilas perpetuate tequila's reputation as firewater.

Fine silver tequilas are as elegant as an *eau de vie* and as versatile as vodka (yet much more flavorful, in my opinion). Silver tequila is a requisite for classic Mexican margaritas, fruit drinks, and other mixed drinks. Premium silvers stand alone for sipping, especially when served ice cold. Try presenting the bottle iced, in a champagne bucket.

Tequila Joven Abocado: Gold Tequila

Mexican legal definition: *Silver tequila with the addition of colorings and flavorings to mellow the flavor.*

This is the tequila better known as "gold." I have been told that it was created for the North American market, and it is not commonly consumed in Mexico. Because of its color, many assume that it is an aged spirit, which gives it a broader appeal, when technically it does not have to be. In this category, the flavoring and coloring of silver tequila, primarily with caramel (also commonly found in other distilled brown spirits), is left to the discretion of the producer. Gold tequilas remain exceptionally popular for shooters, margaritas, and mixed drinks.

Tequila Reposado: Reposed (Rested) Tequila

Mexican legal definition: *Tequila rested (aged) for at least a minimum of two months to one year in oak tanks or barrels; flavorings and coloring agents permissible, as well as the addition of demineralized water to bring it to commercial proof.*

In my opinion, there is nothing quite like a true reposado: a tequila with a harmonious balance between the natural essence of the agave and the subtle influence of the oak. Reposados are especially popular in Mexico. The repose or "resting" of silver tequila in wood mellows its youthful and feisty character, balancing and rounding out any rough edges. Fine reposados temper the harshness of unaged tequila, adding hints of vanilla and spice, and are not overwhelmed by the oak, as are some añejos. Reposados range in hues from very pale straw color to a deep gold and are excellent for sipping, as well as for margaritas and mixed drinks.

Añejo: Aged Tequila

Mexican legal definition: *Tequila aged for at least one year in government sealed oak barrels; flavorings and coloring agents are permissible as well as the addition of demineralized water to bring it to commercial proof. When tequilas of different ages are blended, the youngest age will be designated.*

Aging tequila—the wedding of oak and agave in the barrel—transforms the youthful spirit into a mature and mellow one. A languorous evaporation occurring through the porous wood develops and concentrates the flavor.

Añejo tequilas may range in color from the naturally subtle amber imparted from oak barrels, to a deep golden color influenced by additives or colorings. Some añejos are quite luxurious: smooth, elegant, and exquisite. The complexities of oak and agave and the characteristic nuances of barrel aging—depth of aroma, discernible soft tannin, and soft vanilla tones—mingle harmoniously.

In certain premium añejos, the origin of the spirit—that sweet agave fruitiness—is not overshadowed by wood. Some añejos, however, are dominated by the flavor of oak, with hard tannin and astringent qualities, or are overwhelmed with vanillin, wood chips, and other flavorings, apparent to the nose and upon taste. One asks, where is the flavor of the tequila? The quality and condition of the barrels, the condition of the cellar, and the storage of the barrels all influence the color and flavor of the tequila. An añejo at its finest is not unlike a memorable cognac; at its worst, like a harsh and cheap brandy.

I believe that the best way to drink an añejo is in a snifter, so that its aroma may be savored along with its flavor. Some, however, pour añejo into mixed drinks—but would you pour XO cognac into limeade?

Tequila, like cognac and other fine spirits, does not improve with bottle aging, so go ahead! Drink that bottle of tequila that you brought back from Mexico years ago—it won't get any better!

Tequila Houses and Styles

Cuervo and Sauza are the two most widely available brands in the United States.

Cuervo

José Cuervo is not a fictitious name! José María Guadalupe de Cuervo first distilled tequila, or *vino de mezcal*, in 1795 in the town of Tequila. Today, Cuervo outsells all other brands of tequila and accounts for almost half of the total sales of tequila in the United States. The house style of Cuervo is sweeter and less assertive than some brands.

★ **Cuervo Silver:** Freshly distilled and unaged. Use in margaritas, punches, and mixed drinks.

★ **Cuervo Especial Premium Tequila:** This gold tequila is the most popular single brand in the United States. It is a natural for shooters and a favorite for many margaritas.

★ **Cuervo 1800:** Packaged in a handsome rectangular glass bottle, this super-premium tequila is a marriage of find blended tequilas (reposados and añejos); it is rich and robust, fruity with distinctive oak tones. Its spirited and friendly flavor is perfect for sipping and savoring.

★ **Dos Reales Plata:** Cuervo's super-premium silver tequila is packaged attractively in an elegant ribbed bottle with an ethereal antique-looking label; fruity bouquet, rich, sweet and dense.

★ **Dos Reales Añejo:** This añejo's attractive bottle matches that of the Dos Reales Plata and was originally bottled in limited editions as Centenario in Mexico. It has a very deep amber color and is dense and velvety in texture, very oaky, sweet, and peppery with a caramelized finish.

★ **Tradicional:** See 100 percent agave tequilas on page 31-33.

Sauza

Sauza tequila was first made by Don Cenobio Sauza over one hundred years ago and remains one of the most popular tequilas today, with a wide range of styles. The house style of Sauza is bold and assertive, piquant and robust, a marriage of Spanish and Mexican traditions.

★ **Sauza Tequila Silver:** A traditional favorite for Mexican margaritas, mixed drinks, and punches.

★ **Sauza Tequila Especial:** Sauza's gold tequila for mixed drinks, punches, and shots.

★ **Sauza Giro** (gold and silver)**:** Sauza's well brand; perfect for party punches.

★ **Conmemorativo:** Sauza's super-premium añejo tequila; smooth, slightly sweet, and complex. The inherent smoky and herbaceous qualities of the agave are intact and matched by the well-balanced oak tones.

★ **Tres Generaciones:** Three generations of Sauza are embossed on the opaque smoke-colored bottle of this super-premium añejo tequila. Best for sipping from a snifter, it is velvety, smoky, rich, and resinous, with cognac-like elegance and a butterscotch finish. Bottled in Mexico.

Other Tequilas to Look For:

Tequila's booming popularity has made innumerable brands available throughout America, often under private labels. There is a tequila to match anyone's taste. Here are some to keep an eye out for:

★ **Aguila:** White, reposado, and añejo. Bottled in Atotonilco, Mexico.

★ **Centinela:** Blanco, reposado, añejo, and añejo 3 años. Made in Arandas from 100 percent agave.

★ **Hussongs:** The one in the charming black pottery crock.

★ **Real Hacienda:** A favorite in Arizona; 100 percent agave.

★ **Torada:** White, reposado, and añejo. Distinctive among lower-priced tequilas.

★ **Viuda de Romero:** "The Widow of Romero." Reposado and añejo.

HOW TO READ A LABEL

Besides the brand name, every tequila label will have NOM and four numbers designating the distillery from which it was produced, guaranteeing that no other tequila is in the bottle. The front label will also give the size of the bottle (e.g., 750ml), the proof (80 proof or 40 percent alcohol by volume), and the category of the tequila (silver, añejo, or reposado). If it is 100 percent agave tequila, it must say so on the front label and be bottled in Mexico.

WHAT MAKES TEQUILA SO POPULAR?

▼ Increased tourism to Mexico.

▼ Incredible popularity of Mexican and Southwestern restaurants.

▼ Tequila's bright and lively flavors complement foods. Unlike most distilled spirits, it may accompany meals. Margaritas and Mexican food are naturals and fine tequilas may be slowly sipped throughout many a meal.

▼ People write songs about it!

▼ Tequila has a personality: feisty, independent, rowdy, and fun!

100 Percent "Blue" Agave Tequila

100 percent agave tequila simply means tequila that has been produced from only the fermented and distilled juices of the "blue" agave. Naturally, 100 percent agave tequila is costlier to produce than those made with 49 percent added sugars—most notably from cane sugar.

Discerning drinkers have demands. As more people are drinking less, the quality of what they drink is essential. Paralleling the trend of Scotch connoisseurs switching from blended to single-malt scotch, many tequila aficionados are opting to drink 100 percent agave tequilas.

Distilleries producing 100 percent agave tequila must adhere to set standards established by the Mexican government. These tequilas must be bottled in Mexico, in the same region from which they are produced. Only then can the label designate a tequila as "100 percent agave—produced and bottled under the vigilance of the Mexican government." Also, a government inspector must be on site to verify that the tequila has no other sugars added during fermentation.

Naturally, many tequila producers have capitalized on the trend toward 100 percent agave tequilas (at this time, there is not an accurate test to determine if a tequila is truly 100 percent agave, and quality varies greatly).

The premium tequilas are pricey ($18 to over $50 a bottle). Aficionados may choose to sip them from shot glasses or snifters. I prefer to serve these silver tequilas icy cold. Try them in a margarita, on the rocks, or mixed with fresh fruit juices. Remember, it's not the price and the pretty packaging, but the quality and the flavor. Taste them to determine your favorites.

Chinaco

This renegade tequila, distributed by Robert Denton and Company (the only premium tequila not produced in Jalisco), was a trendsetter. It was the first from the small distilleries to develop sophisticated marketing and packaging to match their premium product. Chinaco combined European elegance and Mexican tradition in one bottle with hand-numbered and hand-signed labels; other producers quickly followed suit. Chinaco's legendary flavor took tequila into some of the most upscale restaurants and bars during the early 1980s, promoting tequila's credibility as a refined and elegant spirit. It disappeared from the market for a few years, but Chinaco fans get ready! As this book goes to press, it is about to be released in the United States once again. Under the guidance of the sons of the original producer, the great-grandson of one of Mexico's presidents, Chinaco's new line includes the famed Chinaco Añejo, with the characteristics of a fine cognac—very oaky with hints of vanilla and spice; rich, enticing, with a smooth and elegant finish. New arrivals will include Chinaco Blanco, with light and ethereal qualities, perfumed with the natural essence of the agave, and Chinaco Reposado, which softens the Blanco with subtle hints of oak; a peppery and bright tequila.

Cuervo Tradicional

In Mexico City at Cuervo's executive offices, Juan Beckmann, the company's president, proudly showed me his collection of Cuervo art and memorabilia from a tequila house steeped in heritage and tradition. Before lunch, we sipped ice-cold shots of Cuervo Traditional (produced in limited edition): a lively and robust reposado, peppery and bright, gently rested in oak with authentic tequila flavors. Since it comes in 375-ml bottles, it's fun to freeze in small blocks of ice which can be passed easily around the table during a meal and sipped from shot glasses (see page 53 for freezing tequila).

Herradura

The tequila with the horseshoe on the label is acclaimed for its estate bottling, natural production methods (including using only naturally occurring yeasts), and pure agave flavor. Herradura was the first registered 100 percent agave tequila and the first añejo tequila imported into the United States. Herradura Silver has a burst of flavor—dry and zesty with a bouquet of fresh green herbs, a sparkle of citrus, and authentic agave fruitiness. Herradura Reposado is naturally golden from the influence of oak; dry, yet floral and herbaceous, with characteristic agave fruitiness, a pleasant bite, and a smooth finish. Herradura Añejo is a rich and natural amber color with a subtle aroma not overwhelmed by vanilla. Dry, herbaceous, and peppery, it also has the subtle fruitiness of the agave and is exquisitely balanced with the complex characteristics of oak.

Patrón

Partners John Paul Jones de Joria (of Paul Mitchell hair care products) and Martin Crowley, a California entrepreneur, market this tequila in slick and classy packaging worthy of "Lifestyles of the Rich and Famous"—hand-blown glass decanters in stylish boxes with colorful tissue paper and ribbons. Patrón is produced in the Los Altos region of Atotonilco in a small distillery in the hand-crafted tradition. Patrón Silver is light and refreshing with undertones of mint and green herbs; slightly peppery, with a smooth and a delicately sweet finish. Patrón Añejo is smooth and elegant, smoky and spicy with hints of vanilla and oak.

Porfidio

Unique packaging put this tequila on the map . . . a hand-blown bottle containing a green glass cactus, at a price of $75! Porfidio is now sold in chic smoke-colored bottles reminiscent of Italian grappa bottles. Porfidio Plata has a surprising pear-like fruitiness at the nose, is smooth but peppery and slightly sweet. Porfidio Añejo has a pungent and earthy aroma, and is dry, with peppery and vegetal tones.

Sauza Hornitos

In my opinion, Sauza gravely erred when they exchanged their old label with "*the bottled romance of Mexico*" written on it for a slick and modern one, but the tequila is still a favorite. Some may be disappointed to know that the name Hornitos is the Spanish diminutive for *hornos* (ovens in which the agave are steamed), not for a lusty state of mind. I grew up on this traditional brand: the fiery and robust flavor of cantina tequila with a touch of citrus and spice. Sometimes considered the working person's tequila because it is an affordable 100 percent agave reposado, it is good in shooters, margaritas, and mixed drinks and makes a flavorful cooking tequila.

El Tesoro de Don Felipe

The tireless energy of Don Felipe, the sixty-two-year-old producer of this tequila, accounts for the quality of his treasure—El Tesoro de Don Felipe. Believe me, I know. I spent a day with him in his fields in the high plateaus of Arandas and could hardly keep up with him—trudging through red clay mud and climbing over stone walls to inspect his precious agaves. El Tesoro de Don Felipe is produced in the hand-crafted style in copper stills and wooden fermentation vats. Like Chinaco, another hand-crafted tequila imported by partners Marilyn Smith and Robert Denton (to whom I am especially grateful for sharing their knowledge of tequila), El Tesoro bridges the gap between Mexican tradition and Southwestern sophistication. It is presented in tall bottles with either a silver or gold embossed agave in a clay oven. El Tesoro Plata tastes bright and fresh with hints of pepper and spice and the fruity essence of the agave left intact like a fine eau-de-vie. Unlike other silvers, it is bottled at the proof from which it comes out of the still. El Tesoro Muy Añejo, aged in oak barrels in an underground cellar, has a natural pale amber color and is not over-wooded as are some añejos; it is rich and luxurious with soft vanilla tones and a good balance of fruitiness, agave, and oak. I am eagerly awaiting El Tesoro Reposado, due for shipment by 1995.

El Viejito

Atotonilco in the Los Altos region is the home of this tequila whose label features *el viejito* (the old man) in a sombrero. El Viejito Reposado is earthy, reminiscent of a clay *olla* (wood-fired earthenware pot) and Mexican cantinas; it is peppery and potent—for those accustomed to the piquant flavors of Mexico. I find this lively tequila a welcome change and more Mexican in character than the sweet-tasting tequilas popular in the U.S. No wonder it's the pride of producer Antonio Nuñez. The rowdy spirit of the reposado has been tamed in El Viejito Añejo, which has hints of fresh herbs and citrus and delicate oak tones but retains a lively flavor.

The Future of Tequila

Outside of Mexico, tequila has experienced an incredible boom in popularity (especially in the United States, Japan, Canada, and Europe). The downside to this popularity is inconsistency in quality. Some producers have been tempted to cut corners, producing an inferior tequila that does not comply with Mexican laws.

Some bulk producers send high-proof tequila in tankers to bottling plants in the United States, where the surge in popularity of tequila has produced a plethora of labels. Although the labels are privately owned, bottles with different labels may contain the same bulk tequila—often of poor quality or adulterated with neutral spirits. These inferior tequilas give tequila a bad name—and a bad flavor.

In order to preserve tequila's integrity and quality, we hope to see a stricter compliance to the Mexican laws governing tequila as well as a stricter enforcement. The inception of new laws to raise the standards of the industry (including tests for agave content) and to discourage private labeling will be the best promotion for Mexico's national spirit. ¡VIVA TEQUILA!

"La Cantina"
hand crafted
metal bar
with cut-outs
of charro
singing
to his
amor...
Jalisco,
Mexico

STOCKING THE HOME CANTINA

Tequila:
el regalo de Jalisco al mundo.

❉

Tequila:
Jalisco's gift to the world.

Tequila beckons a fiesta! Stocking the home cantina with a selection of tequilas, glassware, and condiments is part of the fun. I display my collection of tequilas and shot glasses on a bar that was hand-crafted in Jalisco. Its terra cotta–painted metal counter is braced with hand-painted tin cutouts: a Mexican *charro* (cowboy) with a sombrero and guitar sings while his *novia* (girlfriend) raises her long skirt and dances amid the maguey and cactus.

I always try to bring back a bottle of tequila whenever I return from traveling in Mexico. Labels on these bottles embody the spirit of tequila—bold and macho. Black stallions, wild bucks, and formidable agaves depicted in a rustic manner contrast with the slick and commercial labels found in U.S. markets. Some of the brands popular in Mexico include Orendain, Siete Leguas, Cazadores, Centinela, Tapatio, Viuda de Romero, and Tres Magueyes. (By the time you read this, they may also be available in the United States.)

Liqueurs, Mixers, and Garnishes

Tequilas

Each style of tequila has its individual character. Tequila aficionados collect them in the same spirit of enthusiasm and delight with which wine connoisseurs build their cellars. Discover your favorites by tasting different brands of tequilas within each of the four styles: silver, gold, reposado, and añejo. Many bars and restaurants stock a good selection of tequilas. Some places will allow you to order half-shots—a good way to sample a variety and to determine which ones to purchase for your home cantina.

Keep on hand at least one bottle of each style of tequila: silver for margaritas and fruit drinks; gold and reposado for shots, margaritas, and mixed drinks; and añejo for snifters. Perhaps you will wish to collect 100-percent-agave versions of these tequilas for sipping; they are especially gratifying when served neat, or straight up. A favorite place for a bottle of tequila in my home is the freezer, where an ice-cold shot is welcome during the summer.

Liqueurs

Orange Liqueurs

Orange-flavored liqueur, known as triple sec, rounds out the flavor of tequila in margaritas and other mixed drinks. The natural orange essence in the French liqueur Cointreau far exceeds that of less expensive brands. (For further information, see page 71.) A Mexican version called Controy is traditionally used throughout Mexico. Cognac-based orange-flavored liqueurs such as Grand Marnier or Mandarine Napoléon, although excellent in their own right, may overwhelm the flavor of tequila.

Fruit and Aromatic Liqueurs

Fruit liqueurs in flavors such as melon, raspberry, and peach may simplify making drinks, but they cannot compare to the flavor of fresh fruits. When used judiciously, however, they may help enhance natural fruit flavors.

Damiana, the liqueur flavored with a wild Mexican herb from Baja, California del Sur (see page 71), stands up to tequila's assertive flavor. Licor Cuarenta y Tres (43), redolent of Spanish oranges and aromatics, and Tuaca, an Italian brandy-and-butterscotch liqueur, are also good partners for tequila's robust personality. Licor 43 is a Spanish brandy-based liqueur presumably flavored with forty-three flavorings: citrus and other fruits, vanilla, and selected aromatics.

Almond-Flavored Liqueurs

Crema de Almendrado, an almond-flavored tequila produced by the Orendain family in Jalisco, is Mexico's answer to Amaretto. Less sweet and with a discernible tequila flavor, it tastes delicious in shots, coffee, and after-dinner drinks. (See page 101 for my homemade recipe.)

Coffee-Flavored Liqueurs

Coffee-flavored liqueurs such as Kahlúa, Tía María, and Coloma—a newly marketed brand made from 100-percent Colombian coffee—go hand in hand with the bold flavor of tequila. St. Maarten Spirits (producers of Patrón Tequila) make a delicious new coffee-tequila liqueur called St. Maarten Café. It is less sweet than other coffee liqueurs, yet brimming with the flavors of roasted coffee beans and fine tequila (see page 103).

Mixers

Sparkling Mineral Water

Mexican sparkling mineral waters such as Tehuacan or Topo Chico brighten up many tequila drinks made with fresh fruit juice. They seem to have more fizz and flavor than other brands. One of my favorite drinks in the summertime is a margarita served in a tall glass over ice, with a generous splash of sparkling water (page 73). Look for Mexican mineral water in Latin markets, or substitute other top-quality brands.

Ginger Ale

Reed's Original Ginger Brew, a Jamaican-style ginger ale with a spicy natural ginger flavor, complements the flavor of tequila. Use it in fruit punches and drinks with a squeeze of fresh lime juice.

Squirt

This brand of carbonated grapefruit soda is a favorite mixer for tequila in Mexico, especially in natural fruit drinks and punches.

Tonic

Tequila and tonic (page 89) with a generous squeeze of fresh lime juice make a refreshing warm-weather drink. Some tonic waters taste too sweet; Schweppes is my favorite.

Fruit Juices

For mixing quick drinks, keep on hand plenty of natural and exotic fruit juices in bottles and frozen concentrates.

Equipment for the Cantina

Jigger

A glass or stainless-steel jigger is essential for producing consistent drinks. A standard jigger is 1½ ounces, in ¼-ounce increments.

Lime Squeezer

Handy double-handled metal lime squeezers are used throughout Mexico. Sometimes these juicers, made for the smaller Mexican limes, are not large enough for the Persian limes more readily available in the U.S. Also, many Mexican squeezers are aluminum; you may prefer to use nonreactive ones made of stainless-steel, or citrus reamers made of wood or glass. Small electric citrus juicers are great for extracting juice in quantity.

Electric Juicer

For producing fresh, natural fruit juices, an electric juicer is handy.

Other

Wood cutting board; bottle openers; ice bucket, scoop, tongs, and a wooden mallet for cracking ice. Decorative wooden or multicolored picks for garnishes, fanciful colored straws, decorative swizzle sticks, and cocktail napkins (I collect handwoven, embroidered ones form Mexico).

Mixers and Shakers

Blender: A strong motor, several speeds, and heavy blades are essential; a stainless-steel canister helps keep the ice from melting when you're making frozen drinks. Use cracked ice to avoid blade damage. Most people use too much ice—you only need enough (usually a large handful) to barely float in the liquid used. Blend drinks for up to one minute, or until you no longer hear the ice churning and the mixture is thick and slushy.

Shaker: A two-piece shaker, consisting of a stainless steel cup and a glass, is also essential. It produces an icy drink without diluting the flavor, and is especially good for margaritas. Fill the cup with cracked ice and the liquid ingredients, then attach the inverted glass at a slight angle and seal with a gentle twist. Shake briefly, until the cup becomes frosty, then tap the shaker cup and gently twist it to release the seal.

Strainer: A stainless-steel wire-mesh bar strainer separates the ice (and lime seeds) from the liquid, to prevent diluting the drink. A spring-coiled edge prevents spillage.

Garnishing Tools

Sharp knives: Paring, serrated, and garnishing knives.

Canelle knife: A sharp curl of metal attached to a handle used for making a continuous spiral of peel from citrus or cucmber.

Zesters: Fine and medium stainless-steel graters used for nutmeg, citrus, chocolate, cinnamon, *piloncillo* (brown sugar cone), and ginger.

Dazey stripper: This handy appliance impales a whole citrus, then quickley removes its peel in a continuous spiral. It is indespensable when making citrus-flavored simple syrup, liqueurs, candied citrus peels, or citrus-infused tequila. (See Resources.)

Glassware

Mexican Glassware: Hand-blown Mexican glassware helps set the mood for fiesta and fun. Clear glass etched with intricate designs shows off tequila's silver and amber tones, while bold fiesta colors highlight mixed drinks. Look for clear, long-stemmed margarita goblets, on-the-rocks tumblers, and shot glasses rimmed in bright colors: cobalt, purple, turquoise, or amber. My favorites have bright green glass stems shaped like cactus—perfect compadres for tequila. Purchase Mexican glassware on your next south-of-the-border sojourn, at import stores, or by mail-order (see Resources).

Fine Crystal: Tequila aficionados and collectors of fine crystal will delight in showing off their premium tequilas in elegant glasses and decanters. Tequila looks and tastes beautiful in traditional leaded-cut patterns, like Waterford's, but also look for contemporary designers in your favorite specialty shops. See Resources for some of my favorite designs.

Shot Glasses: Like vodka connoisseurs, tequila enthusiasts often prefer to sip and savor their favorite libation neat (straight) instead of mixing it with other flavorings, and specialty stores now have a range of striking shot glasses. I recently found a sleek, hand-blown crystal shot glass with a base like an ebony pebble that would be a beautiful accent on a Southwestern table setting. Another discovery was a clear crystal cone nesting in a crystal sphere that can be filled with crushed ice to keep the tequila icy cold. I like to mix and match 1–2 ounce glasses: *cantaritos*, (miniature earthenware mugs), an assortment of small glass *caballitos* (pony glasses), promotional tequila shot glasses, and antique crystal cordials.

Snifters: Premium añejo tequila is as at home in a snifter as a single-malt Scotch or cognac. The snifter's wide bowl and smaller mouth concentrate a spirit's essence so that its bouquet can be savored along with the flavor. Sherry glasses are also an elegant way to sip tequila.

Margarita Glasses: The margarita's popularity has made glasses to suit anyone's style available—from dainty crystal to jumbo size or poolside plastic. Long-stemmed glasses are best for showing off these refreshing drinks; the stem helps keep the drink chilled, away from warm hands.

Pitchers and Jars: Serve Bloody Marys and other tequila drinks to a crowd from large glass pitchers. For fiestas, I serve tequila fruit punch in a 2½-gallon glass crock like the ones Mexican street vendors use for *aguas frescas* (nonalcoholic fruit punches). (See illustration on page 92.)

Sugar and Spice

Syrups

Simple Syrup (Jarabe)

Simple syrup is a convenient remedy for minor drink-mixing problems that may arise, and thus it is a must for any cantina. It can take the acidic edge off limes and enhance the flavor of tropical fruits, but will not distract from the flavor of tequila as many liqueurs do. Unlike granulated sugar, simple syrup dissolves easily, lending a smooth texture to drinks. And it is so simple to make! Flavoring it with citrus peel, pomegranate or cranberry juice, or ginger and spice gives an extra burst of flavor to many drinks. Stored in the refrigerator, these syrups will keep for months, always on hand when needed.

To make simple syrup, you need 2 cups of granulated sugar per 1 cup of water. Dissolve sugar in water for 5 minutes in a small heavy saucepan. Bring the mixture to a slow boil; reduce the heat and simmer for 3–4 minutes, stirring gently. Let cool; pour into a glass bottle. Keep refrigerated.

Citrus Syrup

The aromatic essence of citrus peel enhances this simple syrup and intensifies the flavors of fresh fruits without overwhelming, as do some liqueurs. I usually store this in an empty tequila bottle, where the swirls of citrus inside it look very inviting. Use a splash of citrus syrup to sweeten a margarita or other drinks made with fresh fruits and lime, or simply drizzle it over fresh fruit. Because it takes the sharp edge off Persian limes, it is truly a must to keep on hand.

2 cups granulated sugar
1 cup water
Peel of 2 lemons, 1 orange, and 1 lime, cut in a continuous spiral or long strips (avoiding bitter white pith)

In a heavy one-quart saucepan, dissolve sugar in water for 5 minutes; add citrus peels and bring to a slow boil; reduce heat and simmer gently for 3–4 minutes. Remove from heat and allow to sit for several hours; pour into a glass bottle, pressing down on the peel to release the syrup. Add about half of citrus peel. Keep refrigerated. Candy remaining peel.

Makes approximately 2 cups

Ginger Syrup

The bright and snappy flavor of fresh ginger and spice accentuates the exotic flavors of tropical fruit, especially mango, pineapple, and kiwi. Use this ginger syrup in fruit-flavored margaritas, or drizzle over fresh fruit for a delectable, healthful dessert.

2 cups granulated sugar (preferably vanilla-scented)
1 cup water
6 whole cloves
1 teaspoon whole allspice
3 tablespoons minced ginger
Peel of 1 orange and 1 lemon, cut in a continuous spiral or long strips, avoiding bitter white pith

In a heavy one-quart saucepan, dissolve sugar in water for 5 minutes. Add spices, ginger, and citrus peel, and bring to a slow boil. Reduce heat and simmer, stirring gently, for 4 minutes. Cool for several hours; remove most of the whole spices and pour into a glass jar with some of the citrus peel. Keep refrigerated.

Note: An electric peeler called a Dazey Stripper quickly and uniformly cuts the peel off citrus in one long thin strip (see Resources).

Makes approximately 2 cups

To candy peel

Sprinkle the remaining peel with granulated sugar and allow it to dry on a covered plate overnight. Store in an airtight container to use as a garnish for drinks.

Jarabe Tinto
(Ruby Fruit Syrup)

True grenadine syrup is flavored with the juice of pomegranates. Unfortunately, what is most widely available today is artificially colored and flavored, and too sweet for my taste. I have developed a quick method of making a much fruitier, more flavorful syrup that sweetens and gives a rosy hue to tequila drinks. Use this ruby-colored syrup as you would grenadine in a Tequila Sunrise, Sonoran Sunrise, Chimayó Cocktail, or Pomegranate Margarita. You may use either natural pomegranate *or* unsweetened cranberry juice (Knudsen's makes a good one). This sweet-and-sour syrup will keep for months in the refrigerator, and can also be used in sauces and glazes for wild game, or drizzled over fresh fruits and sorbets for a simple dessert. When using *jarabe tinto* in recipes, you can use more than you would of the sweeter commercial grenadine.

2 cups granulated sugar
2 cups natural pomegranate or unsweetened cranberry juice

In a heavy nonreactive 1-quart saucepan, dissolve sugar in juice for 5 minutes. Bring to a slow boil, then reduce heat to medium and simmer for 4–5 minutes, stirring gently. Allow to cool, then pour into a bottle and keep refrigerated.

Note: In the fall, when pomegranates are in season, you can make your own juice. Cut the fruit in half and extract the juice as you would with an orange, using a citrus juicer. Four ripe pomegranates will yield about a cup of juice.

Makes 3 cups

Spicy Piloncillo Syrup

Piloncillo is an unrefined sugar that comes in a firm cone shape (it's named after the *pilon*, a conical weight used on scales). The discernible flavor of unrefined molasses, cinnamon, and cloves gives this rich, dark syrup its distinctive flavor. It dissolves easily in coffee drinks, giving them a smooth texture, and can be used in making liqueurs.

1 cup granulated sugar
1 8-ounce cone *piloncillo,* crushed with a heavy mallet
1 cup water
6 whole cloves
1 3-inch cinnamon stick

Place water, sugar, and spices in a heavy one-quart nonreactive saucepan, and let sit for an hour or longer, until sugar is fully dissolved. Slowly bring to a boil, then reduce heat and simmer for 4–5 minutes. Allow to cool, then discard spices and pour remaining mixture into a glass bottle, Keeps indefinitely in the refrigerator.

Makes about 1½ cups.

Other Sweeteners

Use any of the following sugars in moderation to sweeten tequila drinks or to rim glasses for a festive presentation:

★ **Granulated sugar:** Refined white sugar.

★ **Vanilla-scented sugar:** Bury a split whole vanilla bean in a jar of granulated sugar, and use it to flavor fruit margaritas, coffee, or after-dinner drinks.

★ **Confectioners' sugar:** Often called powdered sugar, this is ultrarefined white sugar.

★ **Piloncillo:** This Mexican unrefined sugar comes in a firm brown cone shape; grate it for use in coffee drinks with tequila.

★ **Brown sugar:** Soft, moist sugar whose crystals have been coated with a dark syrup such as molasses; light and dark versions are available.

★ **Turbinado sugar:** Unrefined, coarse sugar. It is brown, not because it has been coated with molasses but because it is unrefined.

★ **Sparkling colored sugar crystals:** These sparkling sugar crystals come in fiesta colors and are fun to use for rimming the glasses of frozen margaritas and fruit drinks (see Resources).

★ **Cinnamon sugar:** Granulated sugar mixed with powdered cinnamon to taste.

Added Attractions

★ **Mexican chocolate:** Traditionally used to make hot chocolate, Mexican chocolate is flavored with ground almonds and cinnamon. Ibarra is my favorite brand. It comes in hard round disks that are easily grated to rim glasses and garnish coffee and after-dinner drinks. Look for it in stores that feature Mexican products.

★ **Coconut cream:** Use canned coconut cream for pineapple drinks made with tequila.

Spices

Grate or grind the following spices to garnish drinks, or mix them with sugar to rim glasses: cinnamon, whole nutmeg, whole allspice, whole cloves, whole coffee beans, and cardamom.

Salt

Use kosher salt or coarsely ground sea salt to rim the glasses for margaritas. Use seasoned salt to rim the glasses for Bloody Marys.

Pepper and Pepper Sauces

★ **Pepper mélange:** To make a pepper mélange, mix fresh whole black, white, green, and/or pink peppercorns. Grind and sprinkle in Bloody Marys and other tomato-flavored tequila drinks, or slightly crush the peppercorns and infuse them in silver tequila (page 59).

★ **Bottled chile pepper sauces:** Use Tabasco and other of the many available hot chile-pepper-based sauces, including *Salsa Búfalo* or other bottled Mexican sauces, to flavor tequila drinks and *sangrita* (page 56-57). As with tequila, experiment to discover your favorite brand. Mexican specialty stores are good sources for fiery blends from south of the border.

Flavorings

★ Keep the following on hand in your cantina at all times: Worcestershire Sauce, Peychaud or Angostura Bitters, and grenadine syrup.

Garnishes

The presentation of drinks is the first seduction. No matter how good the drink, it is the special touch of a garnish that makes it seem to taste even better—as all professional bartenders know. Garnishes also can give a drink its individual personality. You will find the following garnishes called for in various drink recipes of this book. Use them alone or in combination, with special attention to contrasting colors and textures.

★ Jalapeño-stuffed olives

★ Pickled peppers

★ Cocktail onions

★ Fresh scallions (green onions) for making festive fluted swizzle sticks

★ Cherry tomatoes and/or small golden pear-shaped tomatoes skewered on wooden picks

★ Pieces of *nopal* cactus cut into abstract shapes

★ Whole jalapeños and serranos cut into flowers

★ Pieces of red bell peppers cut into abstract shapes

★ Fresh hot chile peppers (jalapeños, serranos, and habaneros)

★ Fresh herb sprigs

★ Fresh flower blossoms

★ Fresh citrus fruit

★ Other fresh fruit

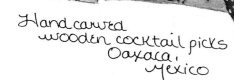

Hand carved
wooden cocktail picks
Oaxaca,
Mexico

Special Touches

Garnishing with herb sprigs and flower blossoms:

- Use fresh sprigs of fragrant herbs such as mints, lemon balm, lemon verbena, pineapple sage, and Mexican marigold mint.

- In drinks, float flower blossoms such as hibiscus (miniature varieties), violas (johnny jump-ups), violets, pansies, begonias, rose petals, yucca blossoms, nasturtiums, borage, and dianthus.

Garnishing with citrus fruit:

- To add aroma to a drink, rim the edge of a glass with a twist of citrus, then drop it in the drink.

- Score skin of citrus fruit in 1/4-inch strips from top to bottom with a canelle knife. When sliced, each slice will then have decorative edges. Make a slit in the citrus slice to attach it to the rim of a glass.

- Cut citrus into slices, wedges, or long twists; using a cocktail pick, twist slices of two citrus varieties together.

- Freeze decorative slices of citrus on a tray in the freezer; float slices in punch or drinks, or attach to edges of glasses.

Garnishing with non-citrus fruit:

- Use slices or wedges of unpeeled tropical fruits alone or in combinations such as mango, pineapple, kiwi, or prickly pear. Make small slits in fruit to attach to rim of glass, or spear them with decorative cocktail picks.

- Use a melon scoop to create colorful balls of honeydew, cantaloupe, and watermelon; spear on cocktail picks.

- Cut triangular wedges of unpeeled watermelon and pineapple; attach to rim of glass or spear on cocktail picks.

- Slice unpeeled carambola (star fruit) crosswise to form natural star shapes, and float in drinks or attach to rims of glasses.

- Make a small slit in the side of a whole ripe strawberry (hull intact) and hook on edge of glass.

Keep in Your Freezer

- Festive ice cubes
- Frozen citrus slices
- Frozen fruit concentrates in exotic tropical flavors
- Fresh frozen fruit
- A tequila bottle frozen in a block of ice (instructions on page 53)

Making Festive Ice Cubes

Dress up drinks with ice cubes in which you have frozen fresh herbs, chiles, fruits, or flowers. Look for ice-cube molds in decorative shapes. Simply fill ice trays with water (distilled water will prevent clouding), and add any of the following alone or in combination. Let the drinks you plan to make be your guide in selecting the items to use in your ice cubes. Once the ice cubes are frozen, store them in airtight containers to have on hand for special occasions. Ice cube trays in shapes such as hearts, stars, pineapples, and flowers further the fun. Try adding a few drops of food coloring to tint the ice.

- Fresh herb sprigs
- Small slices of citrus (kumquats are ideal)
- Small fresh red and green chile peppers
- Whole grapes
- Fresh frozen cranberries
- Edible flowers
- Pomegranate seeds
- Whole peppercorns: black, white, green, pink, or combinations
- Whole coffee beans

Serrano and Scallion Flowers

Making Festive Scallion Swizzle Sticks

Cut the end off each scallion (green onion) to remove roots. Trim green ends if necessary. With the tip of a very sharp paring knife make 1½-inch incisions vertically in the white bulb, turning it as you go, until thin strips are incised all the way round. Soak scallions in ice water about 10 minutes until cut strips splay out and curve. Use as swizzle stick with white end above the rim of the glass.

Making Chile Pepper Flowers

With a sharp paring knife cut chile pepper (one for each glass) lengthwise from the tip to within ¼ inch of the stem to form petals. Remove seeds. Soak in ice water 10 minutes until petals open. Use either green or red ripened peppers such as jalapeños and serranos.

BEBIDAS (Drinks)

Tequila es para saborear,
no para emborrachar.

Tequila is for savoring,
not for inebriating.

When Mexicans gather together for meals or drinks, they raise their glasses and toast with a hearty *¡Salud!* to health and happiness. Before taking a sip they clink their glasses, lock eyes, and passionately acknowledge those present and far away with gratitude, nostalgia, and good wishes. A *brindis* (toast) may be an extemporaneous musing or a traditional *dicho* (proverb), as you will find noted throughout this book.

Tequila: Sip and Savor

Tequila is to many Mexicans what wine is to the French—an integral part of a leisurely meal. Mexicans often imbibe tequila neat (straight up) in copitas or caballitos (pony glasses). Extolling its virtues as an apéritif, they sip a shot of silver or reposado tequila before eating, or savor one between the many courses of a traditional Mexican meal. After a meal, they often partake in the pleasure of a mellow añejo, as richly satisfying as a fine cognac.

I fondly remember a very special luncheon with tequilero (tequila producer) Guillermo Romo and his wife, Lupita, at their family hacienda, San José del Refugio, in Amatitán, Jalisco. Inherited from ancestor Feliciano Romo in 1861, theirs is still a working ranch as well as home of the distillery for Herradura, one of Mexico's finest tequilas. The distillery itself, nestled behind thick plastered walls and fed by a pristine underground spring, combines proud family tradition with state-of-the-art technology.

Guillermo, famous for his pride and passion, had given me an extensive three-hour tour of all the works and the fields, and we were hungry! We sat down at a long dining table looking out on lush terraced gardens. Enticing aromas escaped from the kitchen of Doña Paula, the beloved family cook for more than thirty years, while the soft rhythmic sound of clapping hands promised handmade tortillas hot from the griddle. Finally, lunch was served. Into warm tortillas the three of us scooped steaming *cuitlacoche* (corn fungus), which is as thick and inky as black beans yet has an earthy flavor of sweet corn mixed with truffles. A savory salad followed: succulent green strips of cactus pads, chopped ripe tomatoes, serrano peppers, and onions, accompanied by chunky guacamole. Avocados from the orchard outside, freshly ground in a volcanic stone mortar and pestal made for an unforgettable flavor.

Next, *puntas de filete* (beef tenderloin tips) marinated in Doña Paula's special blend of a sweet mild vinegar she had made from fermented agave juice, sour oranges, olive oil, and garlic made the meat melt in our mouths. *Frijoles refritos* (refried beans) drizzled with a fiery red *salsa de chile de árbol* and slices of *queso asadero* (creamy white cheese) certainly didn't leave much room for more! Nevertheless, to complete our *Jalisciense* meal, Doña Paula delighted us with the family's favorite, *chongos* (a flanlike dessert drenched in a cinnamon-flavored syrup).

Before and during the meal, a server passed a tray of tequilas in handblown shot glasses etched with the Herradura logo: an agave plant within a horseshoe. We sipped the silver Herradura, and the pronounced essence of the agave was as remarkable as the sublime fruitiness of a French eau-de-vie, simultaneously soothing and invigorating.

Later that afternoon, Guillermo showed me a family heirloom, an intricately carved cow's horn. He held it directly under the spigot of a copper still and filled it with crystal-clear tequila. Raising the horn to my lips, I was transported back in time, conjuring up images of Spanish conquistadores, whose Old World gift of distillation transformed the heart of the agave into a quicksilver elixir. I imagined them raising that crescent horn in celebration, drinking the fruits of their magical alchemy. The freshly distilled spirit struck me with an exhilarating warmness as I savored its complexities, at once bold and peppery, yet smooth and slightly sweet. Señor Romo raised a toast to me:

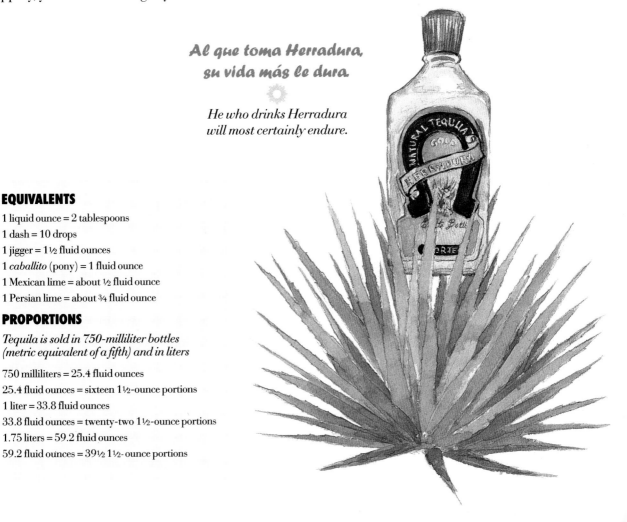

Al que toma Herradura,
su vida más le dura

He who drinks Herradura
will most certainly endure.

EQUIVALENTS

1 liquid ounce = 2 tablespoons

1 dash = 10 drops

1 jigger = 1½ fluid ounces

1 *caballito* (pony) = 1 fluid ounce

1 Mexican lime = about ½ fluid ounce

1 Persian lime = about ¾ fluid ounce

PROPORTIONS

Tequila is sold in 750-milliliter bottles
(metric equivalent of a fifth) and in liters

750 milliliters = 25.4 fluid ounces

25.4 fluid ounces = sixteen 1½-ounce portions

1 liter = 33.8 fluid ounces

33.8 fluid ounces = twenty-two 1½-ounce portions

1.75 liters = 59.2 fluid ounces

59.2 fluid ounces = 39½ 1½-ounce portions

Luna de Plata
(Silvery Moon)

Partially fill a chilled martini or sherry glass with a premium silver tequila, and sip it as you would a premium vodka. Keeping the bottle of tequila in the freezer prior to serving makes it smooth and syrupy when served.

SPECIAL TREATMENTS FOR GLASSES

★ **To chill glasses:** Rinse glasses and place them stem-side up in a freezer for about 15 minutes. (Never place fine crystal in a freezer.)

To frost glass rims:

★ **For margaritas:** Chill long-stemmed glasses. Pour coarse salt on a napkin or saucer. Hold glass upside down, and run a quartered lime around the rim, then lightly twirl it in the salt. Shake off excess salt so that only a delicate crust remains.

★ **For fruit-flavored drinks:** Lightly dip rim of glass in a shallow dish of lime juice, tequila, beaten egg whites, or liqueur, then twirl in a shallow dish of any of the following:

★ *1.* Sparkling colored sugar crystals in fiesta colors

★ *2.* Granulated sugar colored with a few drops of food coloring

★ *3.* Granulated sugar flavored with freshly grated nutmeg or cinnamon

★ *4.* Granulated sugar flavored with citrus zest (lime, lemon, orange, grapefruit, or a combination)

★ *5.* Finely grated coconut and citrus zest (Remove peel from citrus, avoiding white pith; cut into small pieces. Place in processor with 4–6 tablespoons granulated sugar or grated sweetened coconut. Proess to desired texture.)

Luna de Oro
(Golden Moon)

I find it almost a sacrilege to mix some of the finer premium añejo tequilas, camouflaging their smooth, rich, and complex flavors. Simply serve them in elegant snifters as one would a fine cognac, warmed between the palms to release the delicate nuances. Simple yet exquisite!

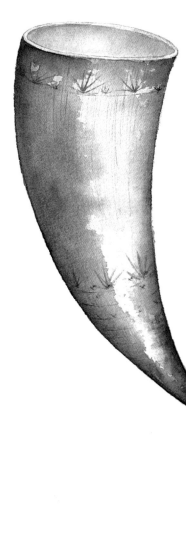

Tequila en las Rocas
(Tequila on the Rocks)

Ice is a gringo luxury throughout the world. In years past, it was never even an option in Mexico. Tequila was simply downed in one quick gesture with a lick of salt and a bite into a juicy wedge of lime.

Especially in the summertime, a premium silver or reposado tequila served on the rocks tastes refreshing. Garnish it with a twist of lemon, lime, or orange peel, an aromatic herb sprig, or a jalapeño-stuffed olive. Añejo tequila on the rocks speaks for itself. If desired, you may add tonic or sparkling mineral water and a squeeze of fresh lime juice.

Una mujer sin tequila es como el cielo sin luna.

A woman without tequila is like a sky without a moon.
—Lucinda Hutson

The first shot glass

Its crescent shape remains a universal symbol of drinking.

Besides distillation, the Spaniards also brought cattle to Mexico. They used the animals' horns as drinking vessels, unwittingly inventing the first shot glass and probably the tradition of downing tequila in one big gulp, because the horn could not be set down until it had been emptied.

How Don Aurelio Drinks Tequila

Estiro el brazo,
encojo el codo,
y de un trancazo
me tomo todo.

My arm I extend,
my elbow I bend,
and without a frown
I drink it all down.

Don Aurelio caught my eye and winked. A silver mustache half hid his mischievous grin, and a straw sombrero shaded his coffee-colored eyes. A bright red poncho with a woven design of white stallions hung over his shoulders to below his knees. Well-worn huaraches protected his calloused feet.

Don Aurelio Lozano, renowned *mescalero*, had just brought a load of piñas (hearts of agave), down the mountain to the El Viejito distillery in Atotonilco as he has done for the past forty years. A shiny blue truck now delivers his piñas instead of the six mules upon whose backs he used to strap the heavy load. When I asked him how often he harvested and delivered, he chuckled, *"Cuando las piñas necesitan o cuando necesito tequila."* (When the piñas need harvesting or when I need tequila.)

I asked to see the fields where he harvested his piñas, and we drove the twenty miles up to Los Altos. Don Aurelio sang softly in a mysterious Indian dialect as we passed rows of agave, a sea of silver speckled with sunflowers and green corn. The agaves are his amigos. Don Aurelio indeed has the keen insight—an art passed down by generations of mescaleros—to decide exactly when each agave needs harvesting. Its base becomes engorged and spotted with purple patches; waiting just a few days too long could overripen the piña, which may have taken ten years to mature!

Afterward, we stopped at a roadside restaurant, where I hungrily devoured *birria de cabrito*, a regional specialty of steamed goat meat in a thick sauce seasoned with chiles and spices. Don Aurelio chose chicken and meticulously picked it off the bone, then recited a drinking *dicho* and swallowed some tequila with gusto. He poured a generous shot, extended his arm, bent his elbow to his mouth and chugged it in one long gulp.

Then he told me his secrets for longevity and virility. According to Don Aurelio, tequila is essential *"para comer y dormir con gusto"* (to eat and sleep with pleasure). He awakens every morning at five. At nine a.m. he has two *copitas* of tequila. During his main meal at two p.m. he has another two shots. And before bed at nine p.m. he has his last two—perhaps with Coca Cola and a squeeze of fresh lime. Is tequila the secret to his vibrant good health? Don Aurelio has had two wives and twenty offspring, ranging in age from eight to forty-nine, and he still exudes a lust for life.

Tomar tequila,
comer bien,
montar fuerte,
y esperar la muerte.
El diablo,
que no se acerque.

Drink tequila,
eat well,
make lusty love,
and await death's knell.
The devil,
can stay in hell.

After lunch, we went to his home in Arandas, down a dusty street lined with connected adobe houses. From the looks of the street, I would never have guessed what awaited us when Don Aurelio opened the door to his home. We walked directly into a central patio bordered by a hay-strewn corral, where a horse, two mules, a cow, a chicken coop, three turkeys, and a rooster greeted us. Surrounding the patio were a few modest rooms with hard-packed clay floors and bright-turquoise walls, adorned with hanging bird cages, plastic flowers, and an altar for the *Virgen de Guadalupe*.

Don Aurelio's mother-in-law proudly showed me her pots of sunny nasturtiums, roses, and fragrant herbs on the patio, while his young wife served tequila in colorfully glazed mugs that she had taken down from nails in the plaster walls. We parted with *abrazos* (hugs), and his wife presented me with a bag containing a delicacy: a candied *chayote* (a squash-like vegetable) cooked in sugar syrup to eat on the long drive back to Guadalajara.

Often I long for the simplicity of Don Aurelio's life, his mysterious melodies, his bawdy jokes. To honor him, his reverence for earth and agave, I raise my glass and toast: "To Don Aurelio, to his tequila, and to the twinkle in his eye!"

Don Aurelio in his agave fields. *Photo by Lucinda Hutson*

FREEZING TEQUILA IN A BLOCK OF ICE

Place a bottle of tequila in a wide-mouthed plastic container, such as a gallon jug with its handle and neck cut off. Fill with distilled water, leaving the neck of the tequila bottle out of the water. Create an artistic display with colorful flowers, fresh chiles, herb sprigs, citrus slices, and/or stems of greenery. An assortment of plastic cacti (available at florist supply houses) and natural stones surrounding the base of the bottle look surprisingly authentic in ice.

Freezing the decorative items in layers holds them in place and prevents their floating to the top; freeze well between layers to prevent cracking. Make the ice block several days before the fiesta to ensure thorough freezing. Before serving, loosen the plastic container by setting it briefly in warm water; then let it stand at room temperature for five minutes. Place the ice block in a Mexican cazuela (deep clay dish), surrounded with bowls of coarse salt, wedges of lime, and shot glasses.

Fiesta Tequila

I like to take the salt and lime ritual a step further. For a spectacular presentation, delight guests with a bottle of tequila frozen in a block of ice with cactus, chiles, or colorful flowers. Pass shot glasses and allow guests to select from a platter of colorful and inviting embellishments: fresh pineapple chunks, watermelon wedges, cantaloupe and honeydew melon balls, mango and papaya slices, and jícama sticks drizzled with fresh lime juice. Accompany these with small dipping bowls of coarse salt, fresh lime juice, and chile sauce. For individual presentations, lightly dip edges of fruit in salt and attach to the rim of each glass.

Los Tres Cuates
(Three Chums)

Uno, dos, tres . . . the ritual for drinking tequila: a lick of salt, a shot of tequila, and a bite into a juicy lime wedge. In Mexico, this is known as *los tres cuates*. Many Mexicans have mastered the one handed ritual: with a swift flick of the wrist, they can savor the salt, tequila, and lime in one graceful gesture. The first shot is fun to try; after a few shots of tequila, however, limes may be flying through the air!

salt
1 shot (1½ ounces) tequila
1 lime wedge
dexterity

Multiply the above ingredients by however many people you're serving. Serve the tequila in shot glasses. To drink, squeeze a few drops of lime at the curve between the thumb and index finger (or lick!) and sprinkle with salt. Pick up the shot glass and hold between that thumb and the forefinger; hold the lime wedge between the forefinger and the middle finger. Quickly, lick the salt, swallow the tequila, bite into the lime, and say "*¡Salud!*" without grimacing!

HOW TO DRINK TEQUILA

I like tequila. And I like to drink it *al estilo mexicano* (Mexican style)—simply straight up so that I can delight in the nuances and the complexities of the spirit. To me, fine tequila should be sipped and savored: it speaks for itself. There is no need to mask it in mixed drinks; instead, sip a chilled premium silver tequila much as you would fine vodka, or an añejo as you would cognac or single-malt Scotch, to appreciate their unadulterated flavors. Show off tequila in attractive shot glasses or snifters.

Que bonito es no hacer nada,
y despues de no hacer nada,
descansar.

❋

How beautiful it is to do nothing,
and after doing nothing,
to take a siesta.

SAL Y LIMÓN: THE SALT AND LIME RITUAL

Salt and lime, traditional Mexican favorites, often merely mask the raw flavor of poorly crafted tequilas. Unfortunately, they also may mask the flavors of premium tequilas. I find them unnecessary additions, even though they add ritual to the drink. Others disagree!

Un tequila sin sal
es como un amor sin besos.

❋

Tequila without salt
is like love without kisses.

Shots:
tequila
and
sangrita

SHOTS AND SANGRITA, THE SPICY CHASER

Beer chasers are popular accompaniments to shots of tequila in both the United States and Mexico. Mexicans, however, often prefer a spicy and refreshing nonalcoholic chaser called *sangrita* (the Spanish diminutive for "blood"). In Jalisco, shotglasses full of sangrita automatically arrive at the table when you order a shot of tequila. Because of its rich sanguine color, North Americans usually assume that it is merely a Bloody Mary mix, but it is colored and flavored with a fiery chile sauce, not tomato juice. Just as the margarita was first made to please gringo palates, the sangrita often served now in Mexico reflects North American influences—most notably, the addition of tomato juice.

A good sangrita is made from the juice of freshly squeezed tart oranges, sweetened slightly with grenadine (a syrup flavored with pomegranates) and spiced with salsa made from the fiery *puya* chile. The resulting concoction, with its sweet, sour, and spicy flavors, is a natural compadre for tequila. Commercially bottled brands exist in Mexico and can be found in a few places in the United States, but they do not keep well once opened, are usually artificially flavored and sweetened, and they lack the puya's sassy bite. One Mexican brand of sangrita, called Vuida de Sanchez, is based on the original recipe, purportedly created by Guadalupe Sanchez in the 1930s at Lake Chapala outside of Guadalajara (although many others also boast its invention). The best sangrita, however, is made from scratch in cantinas and *cocinas* (kitchens), and the recipes are usually well-guarded secrets. Following are three of my favorites, preceded by a recipe for *salsa puya*.

Hand carved and painted devil with moveable limbs by Inocencio Vásquez Oaxaca, Mexico

Salsa Puya

Salsa Puya is as ubiquitous in Jalisco as Tabasco is in Louisiana. This fiery brick-red hot sauce, bottled in Jalisco, gives this region's sangrita its unique flavor, and is also sprinkled on meats and tostadas. The puya chile, related to the *guajillo*, is a dried, blood-red chile about four inches long, tapering to a curved tip. Its flavor is decidedly tart, almost limey, with a piquancy that assaults the back of the tongue.

Because it is not readily available in the U. S. (see Resources at the back of the book), other dried chiles such as the *chile de árbol*, guajillo, or cayenne may be substituted. Alternatively, commercially bottled table sauces such as Tabasco or Melinda's (with a habanero chile base) or Salsa Búfalo, imported from Mexico, may be used instead of salsa puya.

2 ounces puya chiles (approximately 30)
about 1½ cups very hot water, to cover
¼ cup mild fruity vinegar or rice wine vinegar
2 tablespoons chopped red onion
½ teaspoon dried Mexican oregano
½ teaspoon salt

Briefly toast chiles on a hot *comal*, or griddle, turning continually; be careful not to burn them! Remove stems, seeds, and veins; place in a small bowl, cover with hot water, and let soak about 30 minutes. After soaking, place the chiles in a blender or food processor, together with just enough of the soaking water (about ½ cup) to make a thick sauce and purée with the vinegar, onion, oregano, and salt. Strain through a sieve and keep refrigerated. (It will keep, tightly covered, in the refrigerator, indefinitely, and can be thinned with a few tablespoons of water or vinegar as necessary.)

Makes 1 cup

Sangrita Sergio Carlos

Sergio Carlos, the chauffeur for Tequila El Viejito, drove me from Guadalajara to Atotonilco to visit the distillery. During the trip, Sergio proudly and enthusiastically delighted me with descriptive tidbits about the food, flowers, and *canciones* (songs) of his beloved Jalisco. He also shared his recipe for sangrita: 2 cups of freshly squeezed orange juice, 1 cup of salsa puya, ½ cup of grenadine syrup, "así, no más" (that's it, nothing more). Salsa puya makes sparks fly! My version below is pretty incendiary, so you may wish to use even less salsa. Fresh lime juice and a pinch of salt accent the flavors.

4 cups of freshly squeezed orange juice
¼–½ cup fresh lime juice
4–6 ounces salsa puya
1 or more tablespoons grenadine syrup, or jarabe tinto (page 43)
½ teaspoon salt

Mix all ingredients together and chill overnight. Adjust flavorings (adding more lime or salsa) and serve in shot glasses to accompany shots of chilled silver tequila. The drink keeps several weeks refrigerated.

Note: If salsa puya is not available, substitute Salsa Búfalo or other bottled hot sauces such as Tabasco or Melinda's. Experiment to find your favorite.

Makes approximately 5 cups (15 2-ounce shots)

Sangrita Pequinita

In Mexico and the American Southwest, the tiny, round, and fiery chile pequín grows on bushes in the wild. When dried and ground it is sometimes used to flavor sangrita; it gives the piquancy but not the rich red color of salsa puya. The flavor of the orange juice is more pronounced in this version. It makes a lively brunch drink!

1½ cups freshly squeezed orange juice
1 or more teaspoons grenadine syrup or jarabe tinto (page 43)
2 tablespoons lime juice
½ teaspoon dried, ground chile pequín
¼ teaspoon salt

Mix all ingredients together and chill. Adjust seasonings and serve in shot glasses, with shots of silver tequila and wedges of lime.

Makes approximately 1¾ cups (about 6 2-ounce shots)

"Zapatillo" gaily painted ceramic shot glass Oaxaca, Mexico

Bandera Mexicana
(Mexican Flag)

Mexicans are patriotic: they immortalize the red, white, and green of their flag even while drinking tequila! Serve this at your next fiesta.

Per person:

1 shot silver tequila

1 shot sangrita

1 shot fresh lime juice, tart limeade, or Squirt

Serve each of your guests all three, in separate shot glasses. Drink in rapid succession, shouting, "¡Viva Mexico!"

Serves 1

María Sangrita
(Mexican Bloody Mary)

For me, this is much livelier than a Bloody Mary and is great to drink morning, noon, or night. A perfect drink to imbibe while listening to mariachis bellow lusty *rancheras* (ranch songs) in Guadalajara's El Patio Tapatio after spending a day bargaining for pottery, silver jewelry, curios, and crafts in Tlaquepaque. Or serve it at your next Sunday brunch and wish you were in Jalisco.

Per glass:

4 ounces sangrita

1½ ounces silver or gold tequila

juice of ½ lime

salt and freshly ground pepper to taste

½ teaspoon grated onion

garnishes: fluted scallion (see page 47), orange slice dusted with chile powder, lime wedge, or serrano pepper flower (see page 47)

Fill a tall glass with ice and mix in the ingredients. Use a fluted scallion as a swizzle stick, or hook an orange slice dusted with chile powder, a serrano pepper flower, or a lime wedge on the rim of the glass.

Serves 1

Vampiro (Vampire)

The color of this drink gives it its name, and it is bloody good, indeed! The Vampiro is a favorite drink throughout Mexico. Silver tequila, sangrita, and sparkling grapefruit soda combine surprisingly to make a refreshing and lively drink. Serve this for a Día de Los Muertos or a Halloween fiesta.

Per glass:

1½ ounces silver tequila

3 ounces sangrita

3 ounces grapefruit soda or Squirt

juice of ½ lime

garnish: ruby grapefruit and/or orange segments, or a lime wedge

Rim a tall glass with lime juice and salt; fill with ice and mix in other ingredients. Skewer segments of grapefruit and orange on a wooden pick or use a lime wedge garnish.

Serves 1

Sangrita Camino Real

The Hotel Camino Real in Guadalajara serves a refreshing sangrita that is easy to prepare and perhaps more suited to North American palates. As in a Bloody Mary, tomato juice instead of salsa puya gives it the rich red color, while Tabasco gives the kick.

1 cup tomato juice

1 cup freshly squeezed orange juice

4 ounces grenadine syrup (or less!)

4 ounces fresh lime juice

20 dashes Worcestershire Sauce

freshly ground black pepper to taste

1 teaspoon salt

10 dashes Tabasco (or more!)

1 teaspoon grated red onion (optional)

pinch of ground allspice

Mix ingredients together and chill. Serve in shot glasses alongside shots of your favorite tequila.

Makes 3 cups (12 2-ounce shots)

"Calavera Mariachi" papier mâché skeleton made by renowned Linares family, Mexico City

from collection of Juan Beckmann, president José Cuervo

TEQUILAS CURADOS (Flavored Tequilas)

Tequila Infused with Herbs and Flowers

Exquisite gardens enclosed within protective adobe walls grace the Herradura estate. The sweet scent of roses, aromatic herbs, and fragrant citrus and avocado trees perfumes the air. Agaves are everywhere: planted in the ground and poking out of rusted gallon tins, waiting to be transplanted.

On a patio overlooking the gardens, Guillermo Romo's mother, Doña Gabriela de la Peña, esteemed *tequilera*, often serves a special libation—silver tequila laced with fresh herbs and bottled in crystal decanters. The aroma and flavor of each herb remains intact, complemented by the spiciness of the tequila. She serves them as apéritifs or digestifs, each sip capturing the fragrance of her garden: basil, bay leaf, anise, mint.

Fresh sprigs of herbs and flower blossoms infused in bottles of tequila look beautiful and make lovely gifts. Serve them chilled in sherry glasses, garnished with a complimentary fresh herb sprig or mixed with tonic or soda over ice. The intense herbal flavor and aroma will especially appeal to those who appreciate the flavor of aromatic bitters.

Dark opal basil tints the tequila a pale lavender with a lingering clove-like spiciness, while nasturtium flowers offer a snappy bite in peachy hues. Oregano lends its bright and peppery flavor, sage its earthy pungency, and bay leaf (one or two leaves per bottle) and rosemary leave their lively essences intact, accentuated by the sweet and spicy flavor of the agave. Lemon verbena has a fresh citrusy aroma, whereas Mexican marigold mint is redolent of anise. Or add slightly crushed coriander seeds or pink peppercorns. You can incorporate these flavored tequilas into marinades and sauces as well as in drinks.

Making flavored tequilas

I like to use small bottles (6 to 10 ounces) with corks so that I can experiment with different flavorings in small batches; making smaller quantities also ensures freshness. Gather fresh herbs from the garden in the morning, or buy them at the market; rinse and pat dry. Place a 4-inch herb sprig in each bottle and cover with premium silver tequila, which will absorb the volatile oils—the natural essence of the herbs. Let steep several days before tasting, adding more herbs if desired, or removing them if the flavor is becoming too strong. Store in a cool, dark place for several months, or keep refrigerated for fresher flavor. You can always add more tequila (or herbs) as you use the bottle's contents.

¡Salud!
(To Your Health!)

I find this pretty drink soothing and restorative of spirit. I generally prefer it unsweetened; however, sometimes I muddle it with a lump of sugar. When using tequila flavored with Mexican marigold mint, the sugar makes it taste something like French Pernod.

Per glass:

1½ ounces herb-infused tequila
ice
twist of lemon peel
lump sugar (optional)
splash of sparkling mineral water (optional)
garnish: 1 fresh sprig of the featured herb

Fill an on-the-rocks glass with ice, and pour the infused tequila over it. Rub the twist around the rim of the glass, then drop into the drink. Garnish with a fresh herb sprig. For a sweeter drink, add a lump of sugar to the herb-infused tequila before serving. Splash with sparkling mineral water if you like.

Serves 1

Tequilas Infused with Citrus Peel and Fruit

Just as certain herbs complement the flavor of tequila, so do aromatic citrus peels (lemon, orange, tangerine, and grapefruit) and acidic fruits such as fresh pineapple, strawberries, and prickly pear. Long swirls of citrus peel and chunks of tropical fruits infused in silver tequila look enticing and taste delicious. Store these tequilas in widemouthed containers (when using chunks of fruit), empty tequila bottles, or crystal decanters. Use them to enhance margaritas and mixed drinks, sweeten with flavored syrups to make homemade liqueurs, or simply serve in ice-cold shots. Be creative in your combinations: try them in marinades and sauces as well as in drinks. For optimum freshness and flavor, keep these flavored tequilas refrigerated.

Citrus-Flavored Tequila

Experiment with different types of citrus. Select organic produce whenever possible. Remove the peel from the citrus in a continuous spiral, making certain to avoid any white pith, which will make the infusion bitter. Use the peel from ½–1 fruit per bottle of tequila. After 3–4 days, remove most of the peel so that the infusion won't become bitter, but leave a small strip for identification. Tangerine is my favorite citrus to use in flavoring tequila. Try tangerine-infused tequila and fresh tangerine juice in a Sonoran Sunrise (recipe on page 85) and you'll see why.

Pineapple-Infused Tequila

Peel and cut a ripe, fresh pineapple into chunks and macerate (soften by soaking) in silver tequila in a widemouthed glass jar. Keep covered and refrigerated for up to 1 week, then use in blended drinks, or strain and drink in icy shots. Pineapple tequila is also delicious in marinades. A long spiral of lemon peel and/or a split vanilla bean are optional additions. Pineapple-infused tequila makes great piña coladas (recipe on page 86).

Strawberry-Infused Tequila

Cut ripe fresh strawberries in half (make small incisions in each half to absorb the tequila) and macerate as you do the pineapple. Place in a widemouthed jar with silver tequila, cover, and keep refrigerated for at least a week. To serve, strain and drink in icy cold shots or in a Strawberry Margarita (recipe on page 80).

Prickly Pear-Infused Tequila

Cut peeled prickly pear cactus fruit in half (make small incisions in each half to absorb the tequila) and macerate in a large widemouthed glass jar. They will vividly flavor and tint the tequila with their ripe watermelon-like aroma and color. Zuni Grill, a Southwestern restaurant on the River Walk in San Antonio, offers an exotic Cactus Margarita. A huge, lidded glass jar filled with sliced prickly pear fruits and tequila sits on the bar. There, it is always on hand for use in their specialty, magenta-colored frozen margaritas. Use this flavored tequila in my Prickly Pear Margarita recipe (page 80).

Tequilas Picosas (the real firewater)

In 1990, I was invited to attend the Festival Gastronómico in Cancún, Mexico. The Círculo Culinario Mexicano, a distinguished group of Mexican women chefs, coordinated this culinary and cultural exchange.

One luncheon, served on an open patio overlooking the Caribbean, was especially memorable. I noticed Carmen Martí, a stunning Mexican model with black bobbed hair and an engaging smile. She was dressed in summer whites, and the salt-rimmed martini glass she held in her hand sparkled in the sun. As she raised the glass to her lips, I noticed what looked like an emerald reflected from within—a green serrano pepper! When I asked her what she was drinking, she replied, "Tequila Macho" and unfalteringly but demurely took another sip.

Diego Rivera

I have been told that Diego Rivera, the passionate Mexican artist who captured the soul of Mexico in his murals, liked peppers in his tequila. Supposedly, he filled a copita with salsa mexicana—an uncooked sauce of chopped fresh tomatoes, onions, and serrano peppers, colorful as his palette. He topped it with a shot of tequila and a squeeze of lime and downed it in one big gulp. Indeed, it stands up to this giant of a man—a drink guaranteed to connect your eyebrows!

Per glass:

1 lime wedge
salt
1 tablespoon salsa mexicana
2 ounces silver tequila
cilantro sprig for garnish

Rim a widemouthed shot glass with the lime wedge and salt. Put the salsa mexicana in the glass, top with the tequila, and garnish with a cilantro sprig. To drink, quickly swallow the contents and bite into the lime wedge, shouting, "*¡Viva Frida!*"

Note: You can buy salsa mexicana in the refrigerated section of your local supermarket or make your own.

Serves 1

Tequila Macho

If you like this drink, you may want to keep a bottle of your favorite silver tequila in the freezer.

Per glass:

coarse salt
1½ ounces ice-cold premium silver tequila
1 green serrano pepper with stem

Chill a martini glass. Lightly salt its rim. Fill with ice-cold tequila. Make a small slit in the side of the fiery serrano pepper and "hook" it over the edge of the glass so that it's submerged in the tequila. *¡Picoso!*

Note: As a special presentation, cut the serrano into a flower (see page 47).

Serves 1

Lucinda's La Bamba

This is my signature drink for the wild of spirit and heart: a ferocious chile pequín floats in a shot of tequila. Biting into this can be as much of an adventure as biting into the worm in a shot of mezcal!

Per glass:

1 lime wedge
bright red mild chile powder
coarse salt
1½ ounces tequila or peppered tequila (see page 64)
1 lime slice
1 fresh or pickled chile pequín

Rim a shot glass with a lime wedge, then lightly twirl half of the rim in chile powder and half in coarse salt. Pour in the tequila and pop in chile pequín. Garnish the rim with slice of lime. Guzzle it down *muy pronto*, bite into the chile, and you will be singing all of the verses to "La Bamba"!

Serves 1

Lucinda's La Bamba

Chile Pepper-Flavored Tequilas

Although peppered vodka made its debut in the 1980s, peppered tequila is now taking its bow. And what could be more Mexican? The Coyote Café in Santa Fe was one of the first restaurants to feature large glass crocks filled with jalapeños steeping in tequila. Shots of this incendiary brew made many a Coyote patron howl!

Peppers have always played an important role in my herb vinegars. I use them as flavoring and to enhance the appearance of the bottles, skewered within on long wooden picks. Using peppers in the same manner to flavor tequila, both for cooking and for sipping, appeals to my passion for spirited fare.

Experimenting with various types of peppers is part of the fun, as each one offers its unique characteristics. Tiny round balls of chile pequíns, blazing red Thai peppers, feisty green serranos, ripened red jalapeños, anatomically accurate "peter" peppers, and the ferocious bright orange habaneros have distinctive aromas and flavors. I have even skewered dried, smoky chipotle peppers for a smoke-and-fire-flavored tequila, which is especially good in frijoles and marinades.

Assorted bottles of peppered tequilas will be the life of any fiesta, delivering fun and fanfare. In the summer, I like to serve peppered tequila icy cold (straight from the freezer) followed by a bite from a lime wedge. Or down a shot to take the chill off a winter's night!

Use these tequilas picosas instead of vodka in Bloody Marys, or as a surprise spark in a margarita. Whether enjoyed straight from the bottle in all its incendiary glory or in the spiciness it imparts to food, peppered tequila is a bottle of fun and makes an imaginative gift.

Although I suggest making your own peppered tequilas, some commercially available flavored tequilas have hit the market. Imaginative and colorful billboards, advertisements, and howling coyote dispensers in bars announce a brand called Coyote. Although not promoted as a peppered tequila, but instead as a tequila "with the flavor of wild herbs," the capsicum flavor in Coyote is pronounced. As to which chiles fuel the fire, one can only surmise. Mystery seems to be part of the appeal of this new product.

Making Chile Pepper-Flavored Tequila

Look for attractive glass bottles, preferably with cork stoppers; do not use metal lids. Sterilize the bottles if you wish and fill with the desired amount of silver tequila. Just as a fine wine vinegar should serve as the base when you make herbal vinegars, a quality tequila—not one that is cheap and harsh—is essential in making peppered tequila. I prefer using a 100-percent agave tequila in the moderate price range such as Sauza's Hornitos. Herradura Silver, El Viejito with its spicy, earthy flavor, and El Tesoro Plata (although more expensive) are other favorite options, especially for imbibing neat.

Skewer 1–4 chiles per bottle on long wooden picks. The most difficult part is determining the desired piquancy. Remember: you can always add more chiles if necessary. I usually leave the chiles in the bottle; however, for milder flavors, I remove them within a week and label the bottles. After being left in the bottle for a few months, some of the red chiles will become lighter colored, and in the case of "peter" peppers, fade to alarmingly fleshy shades!

Margarita Picosita

When *mi querido amigo* (my good friend) Stephan Pyles asked me to include a drink recipe in his cookbook *The New Texas Cuisine*, this was my choice—pure Texas bravado in a bold and lusty margarita (tasty in icy shots too).

cracked ice
1½ ounces peppered tequila
3 ounces premium silver tequila
3 ounces freshly squeezed lime juice
1¼ ounces Grand Marnier liqueur
1½ ounces Cointreau liqueur
splash of simple syrup (optional)
salt for rims
garnishes: lime slices, whole chile peppers

Fill a shaker with cracked ice; add other ingredients and shake vigorously. Strain into chilled, salt-rimmed margarita glasses. Garnish with whole chile peppers (as in Tequila Macho recipe) or with lime slices. Add more peppered tequila than silver if desired.

Makes 3 margaritas or 6 2-ounce shots

Hot Shots

One sip from these incendiary shots may pluck the heart out of an unsuspecting neophyte, but pepper aficionados will be dancing with the devil . . . or under the volcano with Malcolm Lowry. Hot Shots may bring out the macho of any crowd.

1½ ounces pepper-flavored tequila
salt
1 lime wedge

Pour your favorite pepper-flavored tequila into a shot glass and sip, or shoot and shout, *"¡Ay ay ay!"* Salt and lime are optional but perhaps necessary to quell the fire.

Serves 1

Bloody María
(Peppered Tequila Bloody Mary)

The lively flavors of peppered tequila, fresh herbs and tomato juice make spirited partners in this Bloody Mary—certain to wake you up on a lazy Sunday morning.

Per serving:

1½ ounces peppered tequila
4–6 ounces chilled tomato juice
squeeze of fresh lime
sprinkling of freshly ground black pepper
2 teaspoons Worcestershire sauce
1 teaspoon prepared horseradish
garnishes: chile pepper ice cubes, lime wedge, grated red onion, scallion stir stick

Fill a tall glass with ice. Combine ingredients, garnish, and stir.

Note: Small fresh chile peppers (Thai, ornamental, pequín, cayenne) and cilantro sprigs may be frozen in ice cubes.

Serves 1

Life Before Margarita

When bon vivant Charles Baker, author of *The Gentleman's Companion*, traveled through Mexico in the late 1930s, he found it almost impossible to find tequila mixed in a drink because the locals all downed it in one big gulp, preceded by a suck of lime and a lick of salt. Baker found imbibing tequila in this manner a "definite menace to the gullet and possible fire risk through lighted matches," and he longed for a way to mix it. Of course, the Mexicans thought he was mad. Said he, "It was about the same situation which would parallel snooping around Paris for ways to dilute *champagne fine*, or aged brandy."

Tequila a la Bertita

Baker also mentioned the following drink, which he tasted in February of 1937 at Bertita's; this establishment was across from the cathedral in picturesque Taxco, a town renowned for silver jewelry: "Take two ponies of good tequila, the juice of 1 lime, 1 teaspoon sugar, and 2 dashes of orange bitters. Stir in a collins glass with lots of small ice, then fill with club soda. No garnish except crushed halves of the lime."

It seems indeed that Bertita's drink and Armillita Chico were both precursors of the margarita.

Armillita Chico

This was Charles Baker's version of a tequila drink, a formidable one for sure, and perhaps a menace to the gullet! The recipe comes from *The Gentleman's Companion: An Exotic Drinking Book*, published by Crown Publishers in 1946.

3 jiggers tequila
juice of 2 limes, strained
2 dashes orange flower water
dash of grenadine

"Fill electric shaker with all the finely shaved ice this amount will cover, frappé well, serve through a sieve, shaking to make the frappé stand up in a brief, rosy, temporary cone. When this subsides drink to Armillita Chico, the idol of Mexico." [Chico was a renowned matador at the time Baker's book was published.]

Serves 2

"Borracho Muerto" tin ornament Oaxaca, Mexico

Toma lo que puedas mientras puedas.

Drink what you can while you can.

MARGARITA: Tequila's Most Famous Drink

Margaritas: Mexico in a glass. Salty beaches, dusty bordertown cantinas, and moonlight mariachis are conjured with each sip. This is a not-so-subtle seduction of the taste buds: the tart and sour flavor of freshly squeezed limes, the bittersweet of orange liqueur, the complex essence of agave, and a slightly salty edge. Margarita creation myths abound, most of them born in border bars, where a number of proud *cantineros* (bartenders) have boasted that they originated the concoction. One thing is certain: lime juice, orange liqueur, and tequila capture the romance of Mexico.

The Original Margarita

Of course, I would like to credit a cantinero in my almost-hometown of Juárez (*¡Hay Chihuahua!*), Mexico for the original margarita. Brad Cooper told this story in *Texas Monthly* magazine in 1974.

It was the summer of 1942, when rowdy soldiers from Fort Bliss and "Hemingway-style drinkers who played hard" frequented Tommy's Place on Juárez Avenue. (No doubt, my great-uncle Robert McAlmon often sat at that bar. An expatriate writer and publisher, he drank and caroused with Hemingway and the Lost Generation in Paris in the 1920s and later resumed his drinking in Juárez bars.)

Francisco "Pancho" Morales, the bartender, was mixing drinks for a lively Fourth of July crowd. On this most American of holidays, he created the margarita, the most American of Mexican drinks. A beautiful woman had ordered a "magnolia," a smooth and naughty combination of gin, lemon juice, cream, and grenadine. Having forgotten how to make one, Pancho improvised by mixing ingredients on hand: the ubiquitous tequila, lime, and Cointreau, a French orange-flavored liqueur. Fortunately, she liked it. Confusing his flowers, Pancho named it a *margarita*, the Spanish name for daisy, and a fitting name for the bright and refreshing drink. Because Pancho taught at the Juárez bartenders' school, his margarita quickly became the toast of the town. Pancho later moved to El Paso, married a woman named Margarita (no kidding) and became a milkman, but his margarita lived on.

In Cooper's article, Carlos "Danny" Herrera told another story about this all-time favorite drink, which he claimed to have invented in 1948. He died in San Diego, California in May 1992 at the age of ninety, and to many he will be remembered as the first margarita man.

Herrera and his wife ran a private hotel and restaurant called Rancho La Gloria, which was located on the road to Rosarito Beach just south of Tijuana. They catered to an illustrious Hollywood crowd, including Phil Harris (who later, with Bing Crosby, was the first importer of Herradura tequila in the United States) and Alice Faye, a blonde sweetheart of the silver screen.

A movie starlet, Marjorie King, also visited Rancho La Gloria frequently to partake of Baja's sunshine and spirits. Marjorie, or Margarita as she was called in Mexico, fared badly with any liquor

Hand blown cactus
margarita glass
and swizzle stick
Tlaquepaque,
Jalisco

except tequila. But she did not want to join the men in their macho shots. Instead, Herrera concocted a more ladylike libation especially for her, softening the impact of the tequila with fresh lime juice and Cointreau. Of course, he named his smooth and icy creation after her. Before long, bartender Al Hernandez was mixing it at La Plaza in La Jolla, California, and by 1950 it was the hit of Los Angeles.

Or we may raise our glass to San Antonio socialite Margaret (Mrs. William) Sames, who Helen Thompson credited in a 1991 *Texas Monthly* article for mixing the first margarita. I knew I would like her version when Thompson quoted her as saying, "I don't like weak drinks or weak men."

According to Thompson, Mrs. Sames and her husband idled away the hours in the glorious 1940s at their hacienda in Acapulco, where they "gathered about them a close-knit group of eccentric characters and became the center of an intoxicating social swirl." One Christmas, Margaret Sames concocted "the drink" for Nicky Hilton (heir to the Hilton hotels fortune) and the owner of Tail o' the Cock, a famous restaurant in Los Angeles. Her husband later named the drink after her and had a set of glasses made especially for her, etched with the name *Margarita*.

And yet, publicists for José Cuervo tequila have their own version of the margarita creation myth. Cuervo's story goes that in 1945, Vernon O. Underwood was granted exclusive rights to distribute Cuervo in the United States, but thought he needed to change tequila's rough-and-tumble image. The macho ritual of salt, lime, and shot was not well accepted in slick Southern California bars. About this time, Johnny Durlesser, the bartender at the aforementioned Tail o' the Cock, duplicated for a woman a drink that she had once tasted in Mexico. Supposedly, her name was Margaret (perhaps she had attended a Sames' soirée in Acapulco?). Soon after that, Underwood launched tequila's popularity in the United States with this advertising slogan: "Margarita. It's more than a girl's name" . . . and the rest is history.

You may take these stories with a grain of salt—or a shot of tequila—but one thing is certain: Pancho, Carlos, Johnny, and Mrs. Sames would cringe upon tasting the concoctions served in many bars today, those iridescent green swirls of artificial flavors masking the raw flavor of cheap tequila.

Ingredients for Making Margaritas

Tequila

Traditionally, margaritas are made with silver tequila, which complements the flavor of fresh lime juice and orange-flavored liqueur. Cuervo and Sauza silver have been the most popular tequilas in Mexican bars for making margaritas. For a special treat, try using a premium 100-percent agave silver tequila such as El Tesoro, Herradura, Patrón, or Cuervo Tradicional. Or try the mellow aging of reposado tequilas such as Sauza Hornitos, Herradura Reposado, or El Viejito.

The American palate—with encouragement from slick advertising campaigns—seems to "go for the gold." Many gringos are accustomed to the taste of gold tequila, but I think that the caramel color competes with the clarity and brightness of a classic margarita. Also, in my opinion, the best place for añejo tequila is in a snifter, straight up, or on the rocks. Why hide the flavor of aging? But it is all a matter of preference. Do experiment to discover your own personal favorites. It's fun!

Fresh limes

The key to a good margarita is the quality of the ingredients. Small, yellowish-green Mexican limes called *limones* (Key limes) give Mexican margaritas their inimitable flair. The flavor of a limón is a long sigh, a memory of a margarita tasted on a Mexican vacation. Perfumed from the essential oil in its thin skin, the limón has an enticing floral bouquet and a pronounced depth of character. It is at once both tart and fruity. This delicate citrus fruit ripens quickly to yellow, and therefore requires refrigeration. Unfortunately, limones sometimes are difficult to find in the United States—but are well worth the effort.

The larger bright-green Persian lime, in contrast, is a mere whimper, a lemon of a lime with an acidic flavor that lacks the complexity of the limón. Persian limes are readily available in the United States, however.

Because the flavor of limes varies seasonally and according to which variety is used, tasting the margarita and adjusting its flavors before serving is imperative. Add more lime juice if needed (especially when using Persian limes) or mellow the tartness with a dash of simple or citrus syrup.

IN THE LIMELIGHT : LIMES

To release more flavor from limes, roll the whole limes back and forth on a table before cutting. I like to squeeze them just prior to using; to assure freshness, refrigerate juice for no more than a few days when you juice them ahead of time. Sometimes, I freeze freshly squeezed lime juice to use as needed; freezing it in ice cube trays is a handy way to measure it.

★ 1 ripe Mexican limón = about ½ ounce juice

★ 1 ripened medium Persian lime = about ¾-1 ounce juice

the indispensable Mexican lime squeezer

A Lick of Salt

Coarse-grain salt is preferred for rimming the glasses. I use freshly ground sea salt or kosher salt, although commercially packaged margarita salts are available.

Orange Liqueurs

Cointreau, a French liqueur with a harmonious blend of sweet and bitter orange flavors, is traditionally used to make margaritas. In Mexico, Controy, a less expensive and sweeter version with undertones of anise, is commonly used. Numerous brands of triple secs (orange liqueurs) line liquor store shelves, but remember, the quality of the brand influences the outcome of the drink. Cointreau remains my favorite.

Certain triple secs are too sweet for my taste and lack the natural essence of orange. Some people prefer to use cognac-based orange liqueurs such as Grand Marnier or Mandarine Napoleón; if you are one of them, take caution not to overwhelm the flavor of the tequila.

Remember, there should be a balance of flavors: neither the lime nor the triple sec should overpower or distract from the flavor of the tequila; instead, they should simply round out the drink.

Damiana: Para Subir al Cielo
(To Reach Heaven)

Many people regard a margarita as romance in a glass. Bartenders in Baja, California del Sur, Mexico, like to make sure of that. They often add to their margaritas a reputed aphrodisiac—a sweet yellow liqueur called Damiana. Distinctively flavored by a wild herb of the same name, Damiana is somewhat reminiscent of Chartreuse and is commonly used instead of, or in combination with, Cointreau.

Damiana (*Turnera difusa*), a shrubby bush with bright yellow blossoms, grows in the desert hills of Baja during the rainy season. Mexicans, embracing its reputed powers, drink it before bedtime in hot tea, sometimes dusted with cinnamon, or on the rocks with a twist of lime. Because it is not exported, you will have to look for Damiana on your next trip to Mexico, where it is bottled under the label Guaycura (the name of a Baja Indian tribe). You can't miss the bottle: it's shaped like the torso of a large-breasted nude.

José Pantoja Reyes, manager for more than thirty years of Guadalajara's renowned restaurant Copa de Leche, told me that Damiana was used in their margaritas until 1975, when it was replaced by Controy.

Para el amor,
no hay como la tequila.

For love,
there is nothing like tequila.

Making Mexican Margaritas

Chill long-stemmed cocktail glasses for 15 minutes prior to serving. Pour coarse salt on a napkin or saucer. Hold each glass upside down, and run a quartered lime around the rim, then lightly twirl it in the salt. Shake off the excess so that only a delicate crust of salt rims the glass.

Fill a stainless steel shaker cup with cracked (not crushed) ice, tequila, fresh lime juice, and triple sec. Shake briefly until cup is frosty; strain into the salt-rimmed cocktail glasses.

The following five margaritas boast of Mexican authenticity. They may be too potent for some people. If you or any of your guests are among those people, you may prefer to serve these margaritas on the rocks to dilute them. Dose yourself as you would a martini, with caution! Follow the preceding instructions for making Mexican margaritas. Straight up or on the rocks? With or without salt? The choice is yours. ¡Salud!

Margarita Pancho Morales

Pancho Morales changed professions—from being the best bartender in Juárez to being the best milkman in El Paso. Many bartenders today over-salt the rim of margarita glasses by dunking the glasses in a saucer of salt. Pancho has a more delicate touch: he rubs the outside rim of the glass with a quartered lime, then sprinkles on salt from a shaker so that it does not overwhelm the drink.

Per 3-ounce glass:

salt and quartered lime to rim glass
2 parts fine silver tequila
juice of 1 Mexican lime
1 part Cointreau

Follow preceding directions for making Mexican margaritas.

Serves 1

Margarita Carlos Herrera

Carlos "Danny" Herrera said he experimented with various liqueurs before settling on Cointreau to balance the acidity of the lime and the potency of the tequila.

salt and quartered lime to rim glass
3 parts silver tequila
2 parts Cointreau
1 part Mexican lime juice

Follow preceding directions for making Mexican margaritas. It's as easy as one, two, three!

Serves 1

Margarita Mrs. Sames

Octogenarian Margarita Sames makes her margaritas for those "who don't like weak men or weak drinks." She serves them in chilled glasses etched with her name and only lightly dusted with salt. Finding other triple secs too sweet, Mrs. Sames will only use Cointreau in what she calls "the drink."

salt and quartered limes to rim glasses
ice cubes
3 parts silver tequila (she uses Sauza)
1 part Cointreau
1 part Mexican lime juice

Instead of using a shaker, Mrs. Sames mixes her margaritas in a glass pitcher (never a blender!) with a long-handled spoon, lemonade-style, then pours the mixture into glasses over a few ice cubes.

Serves 1

Margarita Mexicana

This is my favorite version of an authentic margarita. When I am able to make it with Mexican limones, it reminds me of those glorious margaritas sipped in the sun on Mexican vacations, a far cry from the sweet-and-sour versions commonly served north of the border. Be sure to taste before serving because the acidity of limes varies greatly. It's always easy to add more lime or to sweeten it slightly with more Cointreau or a splash of simple syrup.

Per glass:

salt and quartered lime to rim glass (optional)
1½ ounces silver tequila
½ ounce Cointreau
¾ ounce fresh lime juice, preferably from Mexican *limones*

Follow preceding directions for making Mexican margaritas.

Serves 1

Margarita Splash
(Margarita Collins)

Jesus "Chuy" Verduzco Miranda has been making margaritas for more than thirty-five years at Rancho Las Cruces in Baja. Sometimes he serves a lighter and more refreshing drink in a tall glass with lots of ice, its cobalt rim encrusted lightly with salt. A generous splash of sparkling mineral water lends added effervescence to this mermaid's delight.

Per glass:

lime wedge
coarse salt
2 ounces silver tequila
1½ ounces fresh lime juice
1 ounce Cointreau
generous splash of sparkling mineral water
garnish: slice of lime

Rim a 14-ounce tumbler with a wedge of lime, and twirl it in coarse salt, shaking off the excess. Fill glass with cracked ice; add the tequila, lime juice, and Cointreau, and top it with sparkling mineral water, mixing well. Garnish with a slice of lime.

Note: Mexican limes and Mexican mineral water such as Tehuacan or Topo Chico give this drink added pizazz. When making it, Chuy often uses half Damiana and half Cointreau.

Serves 1

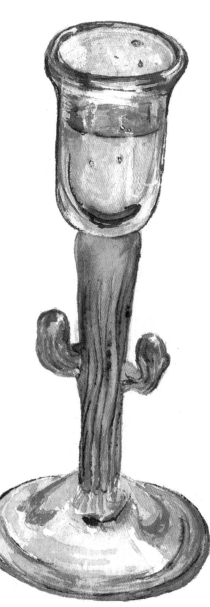

*It's not the drinking
that causes the hangover,
it's the stopping.*

Top-Shelf Margaritas

Some fashionable bars and restaurants currently offer "top-shelf" margaritas on their menus. These upscale margaritas are made with premium tequilas instead of well brands, and they are usually laced with Grand Marnier and/or Cointreau instead of less expensive triple secs.

Discerning drinkers who prefer to splurge on quality rather than quantity especially appreciate the nuances of these superlative margaritas. And tequila aficionados delight in requesting their own favorite brands. Top-shelf margaritas also enable bars and restaurants to create signature margaritas with premium tequilas and liqueurs.

Instead of the silver or gold tequilas or well brands commonly used in margaritas, top-shelf patrons order premium tequilas such as Sauza's Conmemorativo or Tres Generaciones and Cuervo's 1800 and Dos Reales. These aficionados may also call for 100-percent agave tequilas such as Herradura, Chinaco, El Tesoro, El Viejito, Porfidio, Patrón, and Cuervo Tradicional.

Margarita Primero Clase
(First-Class Margarita)

Call your favorite brand and style of tequila. Silver or gold? Reposado or añejo? One-hundred-percent agave? Straight up or on the rocks? (I recommend a few pieces of cracked ice.) With or without salt? The choice is yours. Tasting is part of the fun.

Per glass:

Salt for rim (optional)
1½ ounces premium tequila, silver or gold
½ ounce Cointreau
¼ ounce Grand Marnier
¾ ounce fresh lime juice
lime wedges

Follow instructions for making Mexican margaritas, page 72. (Those of you with sweeter palates may wish to add a splash of simple syrup.) You can also "float" the Grand Marnier as a top layer.

Note: For a frozen version, see page 76.

Serves 1

Baja Margarita

The bright-yellow liqueur called Damiana, made from a wild Baja desert herb, gives this margarita its distinctive flavor and color. Some say it's Baja's love potion. When it's combined with tequila, watch out!

Per glass:

2 ounces silver tequila
½ ounce fresh lime juice, preferably from Mexican limes
¾ ounce Damiana liqueur
small handful of ice
lime twist

Follow preceding directions for making Mexican margaritas, but serve with a twist of lime and a few pieces of cracked ice.

Note: If you prefer, use half Damiana and half Cointreau.

Serves 1

Fiesta Margarita
(Party Pitcher Margarita)

Squeeze plenty of fresh lime juice ahead of time, and this pitcher of top-shelf margaritas can be made in a minute. This is a good recipe for showing off a 100-percent agave silver or reposado tequila.

1 bottle (750 ml) premium silver or reposado tequila
1¼ cups Cointreau
splash Grand Marnier
1½ cups freshly squeezed lime juice
salt for glass rims (optional)
garnish: lime slices

Mix all ingredients together in a glass pitcher and chill before serving. Pour on the rocks in long-stemmed glasses (rimmed with salt, if you like), or serve as icy shots, and garnish with lime slices.

Makes 1½ quarts (12 margaritas or 24 2-ounce shots)

Sweet and Sour

Many American bars and restaurants make batches of margarita mix. They are often overly sweet and artificially flavored, thus masking the flavor of tequila and enabling bartenders to use cheaper brands. Commercial sweet-and-sour mixes are available for home use frozen, powdered, and bottled, but they lack the natural essence of fresh lime.

Upon tasting a real Mexican margarita for the first time, some people may find the acidity of the limes and the high alcohol content too strong in character. They may prefer a sweeter and milder drink, easily made with fresh lime juice sweetened with simple syrup, and far surpassing the flavor of commercial mixes. Citrus syrup adds even more flavor.

Some people mistakenly try to sweeten margaritas by overcompensating with orange-flavored liqueurs, which in fact can obscure the flavor of the tequila and the lime juice if not used judiciously.

Más Dulce
(Sweet-and-Sour Margarita)

For those of you who prefer a smoother and milder margarita, but one still brimming with a fresh and natural flavor, try this one sweetened delicately with citrus syrup.

Per glass:

1½ ounces tequila
1 ounce fresh lime juice
½ ounce Cointreau
½ ounce citrus syrup (recipe on page 42)

Follow preceding instructions for making Mexican margaritas.

Serves 1

Si tomas para olvidar paga antes de tomar

*If you drink to forget,
pay before you drink.*

"Otro Diablo" another devil...

hand carved and painted devil with moveable limbs
Inocencio Vásquez Oaxaca, Mexico

tequila

mezcal

Frozen Margaritas

Margaritas were well known to Mariano Martinez, Sr., who owned a Mexican restaurant in Dallas named El Charro. It is said that in 1971, his son, Mariano Junior, revolutionized the tequila industry when he invented frozen margaritas. Adults took to them like children to ice cream. They were cool, slushy, and sweet, so customers could easily drink more than one. Frozen margaritas remain one of the most popular drinks served in bars throughout the United States. Although seemingly innocuous, they sure can sneak up on you!

Martinez used a soft-ice-cream machine to produce his creation, as do many bars today. Commercial sweet-and-sour mixes help simplify the process. Duplicating the texture of drinks made in margarita machines, however, is difficult to do at home, but try the following simplified version.

Margarita Momentito
(Margarita in a Minute)

This frozen margarita can be made *muy pronto* so it comes in handy for parties. It's pleasingly sweet and slushy, so imbibe with caution: Jimmy Buffett's "Wasting Away Again in Margaritaville" may take on new meaning for you! To achieve the icy texture, divide the recipe into two batches, freezing one as you swirl the other in the blender with ice. Adding a few slices of lime (including the rind) contributes extra flavor and texture.

1 6-ounce can frozen limeade concentrate
1½ cans tequila, silver or gold
½ can Cointreau
juice of 2 limes
2 thin slices of lime, with peel
chilled glasses
cracked ice
salt for rims (optional)
lime slices for garnish

Pour the can of limeade into the blender. Fill empty can with tequila and add to limeade. Fill can ½ with tequila and ½ with Cointreau, and add to the blender, along with lime juice and lime slices. Whirl ingredients together briefly; pour half into a container and freeze. Add a few handfuls of ice to the batch remaining in the blender, and whirl until slushy. Pour immediately into chilled glasses with salted rims, and garnish with slices of lime; repeat with the second batch.

Note: For a fruit-flavored margarita, substitute frozen tropical fruit concentrates, such as strawberry guava or orange passion fruit, for the limeade.

Serves 6

HINTS FOR MAKING FROZEN TEQUILA DRINKS

★ Use ripe, fresh fruits in season. Freezing the fruits first produces an icy drink without diluting the flavor. Peeled and sliced fresh mangos, peaches, pineapple, melon balls, and whole strawberries freeze well. Whole prickly pear, kiwi, and banana also freeze well.

★ Use flavorful Mexican limones (key limes) whenever possible.

★ Infuse tequila with citrus peel, strawberries, pineapple, or cactus pear for added flavor.

★ Keep tequila in the freezer for icier drinks.

★ To prevent diluting frozen drinks, make them in small batches and use ice sparingly. For a thicker and slushier texture, place the filled canister of the blender in the freezer for 15 minutes before serving.

★ Freeze slices of citrus or other fruits to float in the drink instead of ice cubes.

★ Freeze natural tropical fruit nectars in ice cube trays; once frozen, store them in airtight containers to use as needed. Simply add tequila, triple sec or simple syrup, and fresh lime juice.

★ Use long-stemmed margarita or martini glasses. Chill the glasses before filling.

The Daiquiri Debate

Those who like sweeter drinks may want to try a tequila daiquiri, fashioned after a Cuban drink traditionally made with rum, sugar, and fresh lime juice. Because tequila is not as sweet as rum, it makes a refreshing and delightful summer drink, served either frozen or on the rocks.

In Mexico, frozen-fruit tequila drinks are called daiquiris, although they are better known as fruit margaritas in the United States. Fresh tropical fruits enhanced by a splash of a *jarabe* (simple syrup) and the tart flavor of Mexican limones make these icy drinks especially delicious.

Rodolfo "Chacho" Osuna's Welcome

For the past twenty-five years, I have spent a week every May fishing with my father in Baja. We stay at Rancho Las Cruces, a secluded paradise overlooking the Sea of Cortéz. After a sweltering ninety-minute drive on the dusty dirt road from La Paz, the daiquiris of Chacho the bartender are most welcome!

Five homes surround the private resort, one belonging to Bing Crosby's family. One of my treasures is a bottle of Herradura Reposado that my father found hidden away in his fishing locker, left by Crosby, the first distributor of Herradura tequila in the United States.

Another home here once belonged to Desi Arnaz. It still has a guitar-shaped swimming pool. Desi, it is said, liked his daiquiris. And Chacho, the bartender there for 41 years, often made them for him, patiently listening to Desi's tales about the big blue marlin that got away. Chacho told me that Desi wrote the tune "I Love You Like a Daiquiri" for Iris, his second wife, at Las Cruces.

Chacho Borracho
(*Tequila Daiquiri*)

Baja sunsets are indescribably beautiful. The dusk explodes into volcanic splendor, outshone in beauty perhaps only by the brilliance of the evening's stars. I have many fond memories of sipping one of Chacho's delectable daiquiris, while watching a ball of fire sink into the sea or coming to shore after fishing since dawn, sunburned and tired, to one made with fresh pineapple.

Per glass:

½ cup fresh fruit such as pineapple, mango, strawberries, or half a banana

1¾ ounces silver tequila

1 ounce freshly squeezed lime juice, preferably from Mexican limes

½ ounce simple syrup or citrus-flavored syrup (recipes on page 42)

handful of ice

Mix ingredients together in a blender. Pour into a cocktail glass and garnish with a slice of lime

Note: Lime daiquiris, without additional fruit, may be served either frozen (as above) or on the rocks. To make an on-the-rocks daiquiri: shake ingredients briefly with ice and pour into a cocktail glass over ice.

Serves 1

Raspados Viva
(*Snow Cones*)

Street vendors in Mexico sell snow cones flavored with fiesta-colored fruit syrups. They use a simple metal blade called a *raspador* to shave the ice from a big block. My friend Viva Silverstein had a great idea: snow cones for grown-ups, perfect for slurping by the pool.

shaved ice

paper cones, sherbet glasses, or wide champagne glasses

tequila (preferably citrus- or fruit-infused)

citrus or ginger syrup, or jarabe tinto (recipes on pages 42-43)

Simply drizzle the tequila mixed with the syrup to taste over the shaved ice.

"Esa"
Fresa
Strawberry
Margarita

Gilding the Lily: Fancy Fruit Margaritas

Like some of the most interesting people in our lives, tequila has a dual nature. Its unparalleled flavor comes from the blue agave, the "lily of the field". Fine tequilas capture the inherent sweetness of the agave and need no frills, only a shot glass or a snifter to show them off. And yet, tequila, with its versatile and seductive character, also lends itself to embellishment.

In Mexico, a margarita is a margarita, pure and simple: tequila and fresh lime juice laced with triple sec and served in a salt-rimmed glass. But north of the border, "Margarita" has been dressed up in vivid, tropical colors, laced with fancy liqueurs, and flaunted in high style to admiring crowds.

Frozen Fruit Margaritas

I concoct frozen margaritas using fresh fruits in season—mango, pineapple, honeydew, even cactus fruit—instead of the sweet liqueurs and artificially flavored mixes used in many bars and restaurants. Freezing the fruit before preparing the drink gives an icier texture without diluting the flavor. Avoid adding too much ice. Ingredients may be blended and frozen in advance, then swirled with ice before serving.

The quality of the ingredients is essential. The flavor depends on the ripeness of the fruit, the type of limes used, and of course, the tequila. Usually, tropical fruits found in North American supermarkets lack the aroma and flavor of those found in Mexican markets. Select fruit that is ripe, fragrant, and in season. Whenever possible, use the inimitable Mexican limón. It makes all the difference!

When making these drinks, I generally prefer to use silver tequila; its bright and peppery overtones complement fresh fruit flavors. Sauza and Cuervo silver tequilas are popular, relatively inexpensive, and readily available choices. You may prefer the flavor of gold tequila or a reposado. Naturally, the sweet agave fruitiness of a 100-percent agave tequila goes hand-in-hand with expensive and exotic tropical fruits. Keep tequila in the freezer for icier drinks.

Serve these festive fruit margaritas at brunches and other special occasions. Show them off in chilled long-stemmed margarita glasses rimmed with sparkling colored sugar crystals or grated coconut and lime zest. Garnish with slices of tropical fruits or flower blossoms.

¡Qué Mango!
(Mango Margarita)

This luscious frozen mango drink evokes memories of my childhood in El Paso. When mangos were in season, we would peel them and freeze them on a fork to eat like a popsicle. For a special presentation, rim the edge of a long-stemmed margarita glass in sparkling colored sugar crystals.

1 cup fresh ripe mango slices, peeled and frozen (about a ½-pound mango)

4 ounces silver tequila

½ ounce Cointreau

½ ounce simple or citrus syrup (page 42)

1 ounce fresh lime juice

handful of ice

garnishes: sparkling sugar crystals to frost rims; lime slices, and/or sliced, unpeeled mango

Swirl the chunks of mango, tequila, Cointreau, syrup, and lime juice with cracked ice in a blender until thick and slushy. Add more lime juice or a splash of flavored syrup if needed. Rim the glasses with the sparkling sugar, garnish, and fill.

Note: For added bite, substitute ginger syrup (page 42) for the Cointreau, and garnish glasses with crystallized candied ginger and a twist of lime.

Serves 2

Esa Fresa
(Strawberry Margarita)

Street vendors in Mexico tempt passersby with plump and juicy strawberries mounded in woven baskets. This vibrant strawberry margarita will similarly tantalize your guests: the sweet and tart flavor of fresh ripe strawberries is complemented by a bright silver tequila laced with both Grand Marnier and Cointreau.

1 cup frozen fresh ripe strawberries
3 ounces premium silver tequila, or strawberry-infused tequila
¾ ounce fresh lime juice
½ ounce Grand Marnier
½ ounce Cointreau
½ ounce or more simple or citrus syrup (optional; page 42)
small handful ice
garnishes: sparkling sugar crystals to frost rims; a plump strawberry for each glass, and/or twists of orange peel, flower blossoms

Swirl ingredients with ice in a blender until thick and slushy. Add more lime juice or syrup as needed. Pour into chilled glasses, garnish, and serve immediately.

Serves 2

Corazón de Melon
(Heart-of-Melon Margarita)

I named this summery drink after a song of the same name. Ripe melon is glorified in this luscious drink, which is cool and refreshing, particularly on a hot day. Freshly ground peppercorns perk up the flavor of honeydew or cantaloupe swirled with silver tequila and fresh lime juice. Yum!

4 ounces silver tequila
2 cups fresh frozen ripe honeydew melon chunks
1½ ounces fresh lime juice
1 ounce simple or ginger syrup (page 42)
⅛ teaspoon freshly ground pink or white peppercorns
handful ice
garnishes: nasturtium blossoms, lime slice, or colorful melon balls speared on a wooden pick.

Swirl ingredients together in a blender until thick and slushy. Pour into long-stemmed glasses, and garnish. Drizzle each drink with fresh lime juice and sprinkle with a pinch of freshly ground pepper.

Note: Cantaloupe may be substituted for the honeydew melon. Try using tequila infused with orange peel in this version and citrus syrup (page 42) instead of ginger syrup.

Serves 2

¡Puro Mexicano!
(Prickly-Pear Margarita)

You should see the expression on friends' faces when I offer them a "*tuna* margarita." I quickly need to explain that in Mexico, tuna is the name for prickly pear, the ripened fruit of a species of cactus (*Opuntia* sp.) called nopal in Mexico. My friends' expressions quickly change to sheer delight when they see the striking color and taste the flavor of sun-ripened watermelon in this very special margarita. Tunas come in wild shades, from pale green to screaming magenta.

4 or 5 ripe prickly pears (tuna), peeled and frozen
4 ounces premium silver tequila (such as Herradura) or prickly-pear-infused tequila
1½ ounces Cointreau
1½ ounces fresh lime juice
splash of simple syrup
small handful of ice
garnishes: sparkling sugar crystals, unpeeled slices of prickly pear

In a blender, swirl frozen prickly pears, tequila, Cointreau, and lime juice; strain the seeds. Return to blender with ice and swirl until slushy; freeze for 15 minutes before serving. Pour into chilled glasses and garnish the rim of the glass with sparkling sugar crystals and an unpeeled slice of prickly pear.

Serves 2

"Que Mango"
Mango Margarita

Abajito
(Kiwi Margarita)

Made from kiwi fruit, this creamy pale-green margarita is speckled with tiny, crunchy brown seeds. I created this drink for my friend Martin Button, a "Kiwi" from New Zealand and an adventurous cook. Of course, I had thought that New Zealanders were called "Kiwis" because of the fruit native to their country, but Martin explained that a kiwi is a much-beloved fuzzy bird that can't fly. (If you drink too many Abajitos, you may join the kiwis in the land down under!)

3 not-too-ripe kiwi fruits, fresh frozen, peeled, and cut into chunks
3 ounces chilled silver tequila
1½ ounces fresh lime juice
1½ ounces ginger syrup, citrus syrup, or triple sec
small handful of cracked ice
garnish: sparkilng sugar crystals, a slice of unpeeled kiwi and papaya, or a spiral of candied orange peel on the rim of the glass

Place all ingredients in a blender and blend briefly. Do not overblend. Add more syrup or lime if needed. Pour into widemouthed margarita glasses and garnish.

Note: Ginger syrup gives this margarita a lively flair, especially if you garnish it with candied ginger. Kiwis may be frozen whole with peel; peel before using.

Serves 2

Rosita
(Fresh Pomegranate Margarita)

This drink was inspired by the rosy pink pomegranate margaritas served in New York's Rosa Mexicano restaurant. I love serving these margaritas in the fall when granadas (pomegranates) are ripe, popping the plump, ruby seeds into my mouth as I separate them from the fruit. Save some of the seeds to garnish the drink! Freshly roasted Spanish almonds make a perfect accompaniment.

3 tablespoons ripe pomegranate seeds
1 ounce fresh lime juice
½ ounce Cointreau
3 ounces premium silver tequila
½ teaspoon simple or jarabe tinto (page 43) syrup to taste
cracked ice
garnishes: sugar crystals for frosted rims, pomegranate seeds, thin slices of lime

In a blender, whirl the pomegranate seeds with the lime, Cointreau, and tequila until seeds are well blended; strain liquid and discard the seeds. Shake with ice in a shaker, adding syrup if desired. Strain into chilled long-stemmed glasses with a few pieces of cracked ice. Garnish and serve.

Note: For a frozen version, return to the blender after straining the seeds; swirl with ice to an exquisite rosy color. Let stand in freezer for 15 minutes. Pour into chilled glasses and garnish. Pomegranate seeds may be frozen for use when out of season.

Serves 2

Durazno Dulce
(Fresh Peach Margarita)

The Texas Hill Country produces scrumptious peaches in the summertime, giving residents a perfect reason to make these pretty peachy drinks. A light splash of almendrado, an almond-flavored tequila, complements the flavor of the peaches.

3 generous cups fresh frozen ripe peaches
10 ounces gold tequila
4 ounces fresh lemon juice
2 ounces simple or citrus syrup (page 42)
1½ ounces Cointreau
3 slices unpeeled peach
splash almendrado
cracked ice
garnishes: sparkling sugar crystals for frosted rims, unpeeled peach slices, flower blossoms (violas, or johnny jump-ups, look especially pretty)

Swirl ingredients with ice in a blender in two batches until thick and slushy. Adjust lime and syrup if needed. Pour into chilled wine goblets, garnish, and serve immediately.

Note: The unpeeled peach adds flecks of rosy color.

Serves 8

Jardinera
(Garden Delight)

Serve this frothy pineapple drink at a garden brunch. A dusting of freshly grated nutmeg and a flower blossom or a big sprig of fragrant lemon verbena delight the senses before the first sip. Pale green handblown Spanish glassware makes this drink look even more beautiful.

6 ounces silver tequila or pineapple-infused tequila (page 61)

2 ounces coconut cream

1½ ounces fresh lime juice

½ cup frozen pineapple chunks

1 egg white

⅛ teaspoon Mexican vanilla

handful of cracked ice

garnishes: coconut flakes and freshly grated nutmeg, lemon verbena, or fresh flower blossoms

In a blender, swirl all ingredients together except the nutmeg. Place filled blender canister in freezer for 15 minutes before serving; swirl again. Rim chilled glasses with coconut flakes dusted with freshly grated nutmeg. Carefully pour drink into chilled glasses and garnish.

Serves 4

Piña Fina
(Pineapple Margarita)

The sweet and tart flavor of pineapple and tequila are perfect partners. Make your own pineapple-flavored tequila and ginger syrup to dress up this inviting and delicious drink.

5 ounces gold tequila

1½ ounces fresh lime juice

1½ cups frozen ripe pineapple

1 ounce citrus or ginger syrup (page 42)

handful of ice

garnishes: grated coconut/lime zest for rims, unpeeled pineapple chunks, lime slices, red-blossomed pineapple sage

Swirl the ingredients together in a blender with ice until thick and slushy. Taste, and add more lime juice or syrup if needed. Pour into long-stemmed glasses and garnish.

Note: Unless ripe pineapple is available, use canned unsweetened pineapple tidbits that you have frozen in a small container. If flavored syrups are not available, sweeten with simple syrup (page 42). Try using tequila infused with fresh pineapple (page 61).

Serves 3–4

AGARITA MARGARITA

Agarita bushes (*Berberis trifoliolata*), with their bright-red mouth-puckering berries, ripen throughout the Texas Hill Country in early summer. My friend Bruce Auden, chef and owner of BIGA in San Antonio, uses them to make a ruby-colored sweet-and-sour sauce for antelope. This sauce inspired my agarita margarita.

You must literally beat the bush to gather the berries. Place a large cloth, such as a tablecloth or a sheet, under the bush to collect them. Wear gloves to avoid its prickly, holly-like leaves . (But if you do get pricked, tequila may ease the pain.)

First rinse the berries, then barely cover them with water and bring to a low boil; immediately lower heat, and simmer for about 8 minutes. Allow to cool, then strain through cheesecloth for several hours; freeze juice to use as needed. Pour agarita juice with tequila on the rocks with a squeeze of lime and simple syrup to taste.

Frozen Tropical Nectar Margaritas

Achieving the same thick, slushy texture of restaurant margaritas when using a blender at home is a little difficult. Adding too much ice to the blender can dilute the drink. I have come up with a simple idea that produces an icy drink without diluting the flavor.

Purchase exotic-natural-tropical fruit juices and nectars such as guanabana, papaya, strawberry guava, papaya, mango, or passionfruit (in bottles, frozen concentrates, or in refrigerated cartons). Simply freeze them in ice cube trays; a quart of nectar fills two standard-sized trays.

Once the cubes are frozen, store them in freezer bags or airtight containers for convenience. Swirl them in the blender with tequila, fresh lime juice, and Cointreau or simple syrup. Adding chunks of fresh frozen fruit such as mangos, strawberries, papaya, or banana will add extra flavor.

Guava Margarita

Sitting in the lush patio of Fonda San Miguel, one of Austin's best restaurants, amid tropical plants, parrots, and an impressive collection of contemporary Mexican art, you would swear that you were in Mexico. But when the waiter brings a guava margarita, you will think that you are in heaven! Pale pink and sensuous, it whispers of grapefruit, pear, and a bouquet of tropical flowers. Because the restaurant's recipe cannot be easily duplicated in home kitchens, I have adapted a recipe using accessible ingredients.

1 ice cube tray of frozen guava or strawberry-guava nectar
6 ounces silver tequila
2 ounces fresh lime juice
1 or more ounces citrus syrup or simple syrup
handful of cracked ice
garnishes: sparkling sugar crystals for rims of glasses, sprigs of bougainvillea

Swirl all ingredients together in a blender. Pour into chilled long-stemmed glasses rimmed with sugar, garnish, and serve.

Note: Guavas are small round fruits sometimes available in Latin American markets in the U.S. Their greenish yellow skin protects a fleshy-pink, highly aromatic fruit that is floral and fruity in taste. To prepare: scoop out the flesh from its skin and separate the pulp from the numerous hard seeds. This fruit is used to flavor traditional Mexican *ponches* (punches).

Variation: Other tropical fruit nectars can be substituted.

Serves 4–6

WHEN A TUNA IS NOT A FISH

Throughout the late summer and fall, I pick ripe prickly pear from the spiny pad-like cacti that flourish throughout the Texas Hill Country. Tunas are about the size of a kiwi fruit and have a tough skin studded with tiny, almost invisible spines that protect the juicy fruit within.

These sweet-and-sour fruits are seasonally available (summer and fall) in specialty markets throughout the Southwest, where chefs purée them in tasty sauces. If you opt to pick tunas yourself (*¡ay caramba!*), be sure to wear gloves to protect your fingers from the bothersome spines.

After picking, rub their skin with a crumpled newspaper or with a sharp knife to remove the spines, peel them, and freeze them whole in airtight bags for future use. You may prefer to cut them in half and macerate them in a widemouthed jar in silver tequila, which will turn a brilliant magenta within a few days. (See recipe page 61.)

While preparing the prickly pear, you might wish to sing a verse from *Me He de Comer Esa Tuna*, a favorite cantina song frequently requested of mariachis in Guadalajara. It goes like this: Me he de comer esa tuna, aunque me espine la mano. *I have to eat a prickly pear even though it pricks my hand.*

Sabor a Mí (Fresh Fruit Drinks with Tequila)

In cantinas throughout Mexico and the United States, colorful, and whimsical tequila drinks loaded with flavorings, liqueurs, cream, and other liquors, often disguise the flavor of tequila instead of enhancing it. For me, these drinks with wild names—Zombies, *Changuirongos*, *Cocos Locos*, *Peleas de Gallos*, and *Toros Bravos*—have hindered not helped tequila's reputation.

Tequila entra suave,
pero pega duro.

❁

Tequila goes down smooth,
but packs a wallop.

I am not including such recipes. Instead, I suggest making natural fruit drinks, which highlight both the fruit and the tequila. "Sabor a Mí," one of my favorite Mexican songs, was composed by Alvaro Carrillo and popularized by Eydie Gorme and Trio Los Panchos. It captures the essence of love: "*en tu boca* llevará sabor a mí" (my kisses will linger on your lips). Libations should leave the lingering and refreshing flavor of fresh fruit and tequila in your mouth.

Tequila and fresh fruits have a mutual affinity. Exotic tropical fruits and other Mexican delicacies for flavoring drinks appear regularly now in North American markets: cactus pear, guava, mango, papaya, tamarind, vanilla bean, and jamaica (hibiscus flower). Many grocery and health-food stores stock exotic bottled juices and frozen fruit concentrates that are convenient for making tequila drinks. But try using a juice extractor for producing natural juices at home. Freshest is always best.

HINTS

★ Freshly squeeze your own juices from seasonal citrus such as Valencia, Seville, navel, and blood oranges; tangerines; Meyer lemons; ruby grapefruit; and Key or Persian limes. Use them alone or in combination with other fruit juices.

★ Cranberry and pomegranate juices lend a naturally tart and acidic flavor and rich ruby color to tequila.

★ Look for natural fruit juice blends and nectars in bottles, frozen concentrates, and refrigerated cartons in tempting tropical flavors—strawberry guava, guanabana, passion fruit, hibiscus, papaya, mango, and the like.

★ Enhance flavors of frozen fruit concentrates and frozen-drink mixes with freshly squeezed citrus.

★ Use fruit liqueurs sparingly so as to enhance, not overwhelm, natural fruit flavors.

★ Make herb- and spice-flavored syrups, simple sugar syrups, and fruit syrups for use as sweeteners (see page 42).

★ The bright unmuddled flavor of silver tequila highlights the natural flavors of tropical fruits; some of your guests, however, may prefer the color and flavor of gold tequila—or a combination of both.

Deliciosa
(Delicious)

Let your imagination run wild in creating, naming them, and garnishing drinks. Experiment with different juices each time you make this drink.

festive ice cubes (page 47)
3 ounces favorite fruit juice or nectar
1½ ounces silver or gold tequila
generous squeeze of fresh lime
garnishes: lime wedges, fresh fruit skewered on a wooden cocktail pick, fresh herb sprigs

Fill a highball glass with ice, stir in the other ingredients, and garnish.

Note: For a tall drink, mix in a Collins glass, using 5 ounces of juice and a splash of sparkling mineral water for effervescence.

Serves 1

Sonrisa (Smile)

Marilyn Smith, importer of El Tesoro and Chinaco tequilas, has passionately shared her wisdom about tequila with me, as well as her favorite way to drink it: El Tesoro Plata mixed with freshly squeezed citrus juice. Although it speaks for itself, I like to dress up this drink in a tall pilsner glass garnished with a kumquat and a sprig of fresh mint.

festive ice cubes (page 47)
6 ounces freshly squeezed orange juice
generous squeeze of fresh lime
2 ounces silver tequila
garnish: a kumquat and a sprig of fresh mint

Mix ingredients together in a 14-ounce pilsner glass, garnish, and serve.

Note: For variation, try juice from a ruby-red grapefruit (such as Rio Star Texas), tangelo, tangerine, or blood orange. A splash of citrus syrup or simple syrup (page 42), or Cointreau may be used for sweetening if desired.

Serves 1

Magdalena
(Tequila Sunrise)

Mel Gibson drank this on "the morning after" in *Tequila Sunrise*, the movie of the same name. Orange juice swirled with grenadine and tequila capture the glowing colors of a Southwestern sunrise in this drink. My version is made with freshly squeezed orange juice and less grenadine than in sweeter versions. It makes an especially festive fall drink when served in a pilsner glass filled with ice cubes that have been frozen with pomegranate seeds—they look like rubies encrusted in ice.

festive ice cubes (page 47)
2 ounces gold tequila, or orange peel-infused tequila (page 61)
4 ounces freshly squeezed orange juice
1 ounce fresh lime juice (or more if desired)
1 teaspoon grenadine (slightly more if using jarabe tinto, page 43)
splash of Cointreau (optional)
garnishes: orange slice, sprig of fresh mint

Fill a 12–14-ounce pilsner glass with festive ice cubes. Add tequila, orange juice, and lime, stirring well; float the grenadine. Garnish and serve immediately.

Note: Substitute ¼ ounce of almendrado for the grenadine. For a *Madrugada* (Tequila Sunset), simply swirl the following ingredients in a blender with a small handful of ice, and pour into a highball glass: 1½ ounces tequila, 1½ ounces orange juice, ½ slice orange with peel, and 1–2 teaspoons grenadine syrup.

Serves 1

Sonoran Sunrise

When Mark Haughen isn't "lost in the rain in Veracruz" (as we once were when driving in search of Mexican cookbook author Patricia Quintana's ranch), he's creating Southwestern delectables at Tejas Restaurant in Minneapolis, playing the guitar, or sipping a Sonoran Sunrise, one of Tejas' specialties. It also makes a festive holiday drink.

handful of ice
1½ ounces tequila añejo, tangerine or prickly pear–infused tequila (page 61)
8 ounces fresh tangerine juice
½ ounce Grand Marnier
½ ounce cactus pear purée

Fill a 12-ounce glass with ice. Pour in the tequila and tangerine juice. Drizzle Grand Marnier and cactus pear purée over the top .

Note: To make cactus pear purée, whirl peeled cactus fruit in a blender; strain out the seeds.

Serves 1

Tequilada
(Piña Colada with Tequila)

There's nothing like a piña colada and a good soak in the sun on the Playa de Ropa in Zihuatañejo on the Pacific coast of Mexico—or in your own backyard. The delicious drink is extra special when sipped from *popotes* (straws) in a hollowed-out fresh pineapple. Tequila brightens the fruity flavors and is not as sweet as the rum traditionally used in piña coladas.

1 fresh pineapple
2 ounces silver tequila
2 ounces gold tequila or pineapple-infused tequila (page 61)
4 ounces chilled pineapple juice
2 ounces cream of coconut (coconut milk)
½ cup fresh pineapple chunks, frozen
1 ounce fresh lime juice
⅛ teaspoon vanilla extract, preferably Mexican
cracked ice
garnish: a fresh pineapple chunk and a wedge of lime per glass; fresh hibiscus or orchids, fresh pineapple sage in bloom

Cut the top off the pineapple, leaving its leaves intact. Scoop out the pulp, leaving a ¾-inch shell. Chill the pineapple shell and top; freeze pineapple pulp until ready to use. Whirl all remaining ingredients in a blender with cracked ice until thick and slushy. Pour into chilled pineapple shell; garnish, and sip through fancy straws with someone special.

Serves 2

Viva España
(Spanish Cooler)

Many people think of tequila as strictly a summer drink. But this drink, rich and regal in its purple hues, salutes autumn's glory. Pomegranates, oranges, and grapes—gifts from Spain to the New World—mingle deliciously with tequila. For a special effect, freeze purple grapes and pomegranate seeds in ice cubes and serve in a pilsner glass.

4 ounces pomegranate juice
2 ounces freshly squeezed orange juice
½ ounce freshly squeezed lime juice
1½ ounces silver tequila or orange peel-infused tequila (page 61)
splash of grenadine syrup for color
garnish for rim of glass: a cluster of three purple grapes, sprig of cinnamon basil

Fill a wine goblet with ice. Use a reamer to extract juice from halves of pomegranates, or purchase juice in health-food or Middle Eastern food stores. Add juices and tequila and stir; garnish and serve.

Serves 1

Flor de Jamaica
(ha-MY-cuh—Hibiscus Flower Cooler)

A ruby-colored agua fresca (non-alcoholic fruit drink) served by street vendors in Mexico from large glass jars inspired this lovely drink. Made from *flor de jamaica* (dried hibiscus blossoms), it has a decidedly tart and fruity flavor reminiscent of sour cherries and cranberries with floral undertones. It is a natural for tequila! Although commercially bottled brands of hibiscus punch are available, it's fun to make your own. I grow this tropical hibiscus in my garden; its leaves and blossoms are a regal ruby color. You can purchase dried blossoms in health food stores.

4 ounces flor de jamaica punch (recipe follows)
1½ ounces silver tequila
squeeze of fresh lime
generous sprinkling of jamaica flowers
splash of mineral water (optional)
garnish: lime wedge or orange slice

Mix ingredients together and serve in a tall glass (I use tall pilsner glasses) with lots of ice and a liberal sprinkling of jamaica blossoms reserved from the punch; garnish and serve.

Serves 1

Flor de Jamaica Punch
(Hibiscus Punch)

In a 2-quart stainless steel or enamel pan, combine 2 cups dried jamaica blossoms with 6 cups water and 1 cup sugar; bring to a slow boil. Reduce heat and simmer for about 3 minutes; let cool. Pour into a glass pitcher; chill several hours or overnight. Reserve the blossoms for garnish. Keeps for several days refrigerated.

Makes 1 quart

Blue Weber

I named this drink after the species of the agave from which tequila is made. It reminds me of the azure rows of agave shimmering in the Jalisco sunshine. A combination of freshly squeezed grapefruit juice and tequila make this a cooling summer drink.

1½ ounces premium silver tequila
slpash blue curaçao
3 ounces freshly squeezed grapefruit juice
cracked ice
garnish: twist of grapefruit peel

Mix ingredients together and serve in a long-stemmed glass filled with cracked ice. Garnish with a twist of fresh grapefruit peel.

Serves 1

Chimayó Cocktail
(New Mexico Apple Cider Spiked With Tequila)

You can make this drink at home, but you cannot duplicate the crisp fall air, the pungent aroma of dried-chile clusters hanging in *ristras* to dry, or the enchanting vista from the patio of Rancho Chimayó, the popular restaurant 40 miles north of Santa Fe. There they serve this specialty drink made from locally pressed apple cider laced with gold tequila, lemon juice, and crème de cassis. In my version, a splash of jarabe tinto replaces the cassis, giving the drink a rosy blush.

3 ounces Cuervo Especial (gold tequila)
2 ounces apple cider (or fresh juice extracted with a juicer from tart apples)
½ ounce jarabe tinto (page 43) or crème de cassis
½ ounce lemon juice

Combine all ingredients in a shaker with ice; shake vigorously. Strain into a chilled glass and garnish with an apple slice and a sprig of fresh mint.

Serves 2

Pique
(Spicy Orange and Tequila Perk)

In Guadalajara, the cantina El Pueblito in the Hyatt Regency is a wonderful place to hear mariachis. More than twenty talented young men in suited regalia— sons of Guadalajara's finest mariachis—entertain from a stage while patrons passionately sing along. Surprisingly, it is a hangout for locals, and few of the guests in the hotel realize it exists. (Don't miss it!) It is there that Inez Flores makes delicious *botanas* (appetizers) from her open kitchen, patting out tortillas for the *tacos al pastor* (roasted meat tacos). Quesadillas of creamy melted cheese embellished with *flores de calabasa* (squash blossoms) are accentuated by her spicy salsas.

Mario Quiroz, one of the bartenders, introduced me to this feisty drink, a favorite of the lively crowd there. Pique owes its piquancy to fresh orange juice spiked with tequila and a generous splash of Tabasco and grenadine. Move over, Bloody Mary! This makes the quintessential brunch drink. Show off its pretty peach color in tall glasses, or make it by the pitcher.

For each serving:

1½ ounces tequila
4 ounces fresh orange juice
squeeze of fresh lime (½ Mexican lime)
generous splash of Tabasco
½ teaspoon grenadine
ice
garnishes: finely chopped red onion, whole green or red jalapeño flower (page 47) hooked on side of glass, or scallion swizzle stick (see page 47)

Mix all ingredients together in a tall glass with lots of ice, garnish, and serve with a wink and a smile.

Note: Try omitting the Tabasco and using chile pepper-flavored tequila instead. (See page 64.) Also, try substituting pineapple juice for the orange juice. Freeze small red and green chile peppers in ice cubes to embellish this drink.

Serves 1

Hand painted
papier mâché
devil
from Celaya,
Guanajuato

MIXERS AND SHAKERS:
Classic Cocktails with a Tequila Twist

M. F. K. Fisher wrote passionately about the celebration of life with food and friends. No wonder she was a tequila aficionada! She ranked it with vodka as "the two most appetizing firewaters in the world" (from *The Art of Eating*). Although tequila speaks for itself in a shot glass or a snifter, its complex and intriguing flavor also mixes well.

Here are some favorites.

TNT
(Tequila and Tonic)

Guillermo Romo, producer of tequila Herradura, first made this drink for me. TNT is a light and refreshing summer concoction. Using a premium 100 percent agave silver or añejo tequila, or Herradura Reposado, gives the drink its special character.

lime twist to rim glass
1½ ounce tequila
ice
tonic
garnish: a twist of lime

Rim a highball glass with the lime twist. Pour the tequila over the ice in the glass; fill with tonic. Garnish with twist of lime.

Note: For an aromatic burst of flavor, substitute an herb-infused silver tequila (page 59).

Serves 1

Tequini
(Tequila Martini)

A premium silver tequila will give any vodka or gin competition in this upscale Mexican martini.

Per serving:

1½ ounces premium silver tequila
½ ounce dry vermouth
cracked ice
**garnish: twist of lime peel or a
    jalapeño-stuffed olive**

Pour tequila and vermouth over ice in a mixing glass. Stir briefly until chilled. Strain ice and pour immediately into chilled 3-ounce martini glass and garnish.

Note: Substitute herb-infused tequila for the vermouth if desired (page 59) or use half sweet vermouth and half dry vermouth for a medium tequini.

Serves 1

Blue Agave Mist

This cool and shimmery drink shows off a 100 percent agave tequila just as a Scotch mist highlights a single-malt Scotch. It's perfect for sipping while watching a Southwestern sunset—when you can't be by the sea in Mexico.

Per serving:

twist of lime
crushed ice
1½–2 ounces premium silver or añejo tequila

Rim the edge of an old-fashion glass with the lime twist, and fill with crushed ice. Add the tequila and the twist of lime.

Serves 1

Mexican Mermaid
(Champagne Cocktail)

Throughout Mexico, even in the highlands far from the sea, Indian artists have an infatuation with mermaids. They paint them, they carve them, they mold them from clay. For the past three years, I have visited Michoacán, Mexico, for the Día de los Muertos (Day of the Dead). On my last trip, I was honored to become the godmother of a Tarascan Indian baby boy, José María, from the village of Ocumicho. His grandfather, Emilio Basilio, his grandmother, María, and his father Estevan, are world renowned for their brightly painted clay figures: devils, Christ figures, virgins, and mermaids, of which I have quite a collection.

In Mexico, mermaids (*sirenas*) represent temptation, enticing desire and carnal sin. Naturally, I had to create a drink worthy of such allure: a cool combination of two of my favorites, premium silver tequila and champagne. This shimmering and seductive cocktail is certain to make a splash at any party.

per serving:

1 triangular chunk of fresh pineapple, generously dusted with sparkling colored-sugar crystals
1 ounce premium silver tequila, chilled
dry and fruity champagne, chilled
splash of blue Curaçao
long twist of lime peel, preferably spiral cut

Attach sugar-coated pineapple chunk to the rim of a champagne flute glass. Add tequila and fill the glass with champagne, adding the blue Curaçao and a spiral of lime peel, and serve immediately. Tell guests to drop the pineapple chunk into the drink for an added splash of bubbles.

Serves 1

Zona Rosa
(Pink Zone)

Rosy pink as its name implies, this Mexican Manhattan is as at home in Mexico City's trendy nightspot strip, La Zona Rosa, as it is in New York's lively Manhattan.

Per serving:

ice
1½ ounces tequila añejo
¾ ounce sweet vermouth
2 dashes Peychaud or Angostura bitters
twist of orange peel

Into a mixing glass filled with ice, pour the tequila, vermouth, and bitters. Stir until chilled; strain into a chilled cocktail glass, or serve on the rocks with a twist of orange peel.

Note: Substitute dry vermouth for a less sweet drink, or use an herb-infused tequila.

Serves 1

"Sirenas Crudas" Hungover Mermaids painted coconut shells with molded plaster mermaids Xalitla, Guerrero

Pepino
(Jamaican-Style Ginger Ale and Añejo)

The Fourth of July in Texas is usually hot as firecrackers. I created this drink, using ingredients on hand, to beat the heat while camping on the Llano River. The bright and peppery flavor of Jamaican-style ginger ale complements the lively flavor of tequila. Adding two slices of cucumber, along with lots of ice and a squeeze of fresh lime, makes this summer drink extra refreshing. (You have trusted me so far, haven't you?)

Per serving:

twist of lime peel
1½ ounces tequila añejo
generous splash of Reed's Original Ginger Brew
2 cucumber slices
squeeze of fresh lime juice
ice

Rub twist of lime peel along rim of glass. Mix ingredients together and serve with lots of ice. Eat the ice-cold cucumber slices and make another drink!

Serves 1

Los niños y los borrachos dicen la verdad.

❋

Drunkards and children can't tell a lie.

"Los Borrachos"
The Drunkards
hand carved and
painted animals
drinking mezcal
by Inocencio
Vasquez
San Martin
Tilcajete,
Oaxaca

La tarde está tequilera.

❋

It's a tequila afternoon.

"Fiesta Ponche"
in an agua
fresca jar

FIESTA PONCHES: Punches with a Punch

Mexican street vendors proffer nonalcoholic fruit punches from their stalls, enticingly displayed in large, lidded jars of clear glass. These punches glisten in the sun, candy-colored and filled with chunks of tropical fruits: *sandía* (watermelon), *melón* (cantaloupe), *coco* (coconut), papaya, *jamaica* (hibiscus flowers), mango, and *tamarindo* (tamarind pod). These *aguas frescas* have been an inspiration for the tequila *ponches* (punches) that have become my signature presentations for festive occasions. They showcase tequila in a fresh and unexpected way.

Too often, guests dread the common-variety party punch, which evokes images of cloying concoctions devised to stretch and mask the flavor of inexpensive brands of liquor. Instead, I delight guests with refreshing ponches bursting with flavor and color, offering visual as well as gustatory delight. They turn parties into very special occasions. And because guests can (and do) serve themselves, I am free to mingle and have a good time.

Few people would believe that tequila is the magical secret ingredient in these party punches, brightening and balancing the flavors of tropical fruits, citrus, and spice.

HIGHLIGHT OF THE FIESTA

I purchased one of the large, lidded agua fresca jars at a Mexican hardware store specifically for making my punches. Look for similar ones in import and specialty stores in the United States as well. A large glass punch bowl can serve as an alternative. The clear glass reflects in jewel-like splendor the wedges of tropical fruits, the colorful flowers, and the sprigs of fresh green herbs that I use to flavor my creations.

Wreathe the base of the jar or punch bowl with clusters of red and green grapes, hibiscus flowers, orchids, plump whole strawberries, kumquats, tropical fruits, and sprays of greenery for a spectacular centerpiece. Decorative ice cubes in an ice bucket will further enhance the fiesta mood.

Cazuela Guadalajara
(Guadalajara Punch)

Throughout Jalisco, this refreshing drink is served in large, wide-mouthed clay bowls, called *cazuelas*, so that the citrus wedges in it may be picked up and eaten or squeezed into the drink. Mexicans pop chunks of watermelon and fresh pineapple into their mouths and sip the tequila-laced libation through a straw. I present this punch in a large glass jar which shows off all the colorful fruits and serve it in long-stemmed jumbo margarita glasses or soup bowls filled with cracked ice, alternatives for cazuelas. A guest once called this drink "the quintessential finger bowl," I call it the "the ultimate fruit cocktail". Make sure that guests get plenty of the spiked watermelon and pineapple!

½ watermelon, (about 8 pounds) cut into bite-sized chunks or triangles
1 fresh pineapple, cut into bite-sized chunks
1 liter bottle silver tequila
2 cups gold tequila
4 oranges, cut into wedges
2 lemons, sliced
6 limes, quartered
3 small ruby grapefruit, cut in wedges
4 cups fresh orange juice
3 star fruit sliced into star shapes
½ cup lime juice
1 can (46 ounces) unsweetened pineapple juice
3 cans (12 ounces each) Squirt

Place the watermelon and pineapple in a 2 gallon widemouthed glass jar and add the tequila, the juices, the oranges, lemons and star fruit. Chill for 6-8 hours, stirring occasionally, adding the grapefruit and limes a few hours before serving. Serve in widemouthed glasses or bowls filled with cracked ice, a generous splash of Squirt, and a straw.

Makes approximately 20 servings

Note: the flavor of this punch improves with age. It will keep several days in the refrigerator; the watermelon, however, will lose its texture. Add more fruit if desired.

Ponche de Manzana
(Spicy Apple Punch with Pomegranate Seeds)

The aroma of hot mulled cider simmering on the stove is one that I long for in the autumn. Often, however, the mild Southwestern climate does not cooperate and an iced drink is more inviting. This punch makes a festive alternative to hot cider, paying tribute to autumn's glory—tart, green apples, fresh mint, crimson pomegranate seeds, cinnamon and spice. Spiking it with tequila instead of the sweeter and more traditional rum makes it especially bright and refreshing.

1 gallon unsweetened apple juice
3 tablespoons Mulled Spice Mix (recipe follows)
6 3-inch cinnamon sticks
1½ cups golden raisins
4 lemons, sliced
2 large bunches fresh mint
3 green apples (Granny Smith), cut into small chunks
2 red apples, cut into small chunks
juice of 3 lemons
1 liter gold tequila
2–3 bottles (12 fl. oz. each) Reed's Original Ginger Brew or Spiced Apple Brew, or ginger ale
1 pomegranate, seeds removed and saved
garnishes: cinnamon sugar to rim glasses, mint sprigs or marigold mint with its bright yellow blossoms

Pour 8 cups of the apple juice into a small saucepan; add the mulled spice, cinnamon sticks, raisins, and slices of 1 lemon. Bring to boil, then reduce heat and simmer for 15 minutes. Allow to cool; strain, reserving cinnamon sticks and raisins. Pour into a 2½-gallon glass jar with the remaining apple juice, cinnamon sticks, raisins, sliced lemons, and fresh mint sprigs. Sprinkle the apple chunks with the juice of 1 lemon and add them, along with the remaining lemon juice. Add the bottle of tequila and allow to mellow for at least six hours or overnight. Just prior to serving, add the ginger ale or apple cider for effervescence. Serve in goblets rimmed with cinnamon sugar, with plenty of the spiked apples and pomegranate seeds in each glass. Garnish with a sprig of mint or marigold mint with its bright yellow blossoms, and serve.

Note: For Mulled Spice mixture, combine 1 tablespoon each whole allspice and whole coriander, 1 teaspoon each whole cloves, whole anise seeds, and grated nutmeg, and 2 bay leaves. To serve hot: bring punch ingredients except tequila and ginger ale to a boil; reduce heat and simmer for 30 minutes. Pour into mugs and spike with a shot of gold tequila (I prefer using unfiltered apple juice for this version).

Makes approximately 25 servings

star fruit

Verano Tropical
(Tropical Summer Punch)

Exotic and exceptionally refreshing, this punch is perfect for a sultry summer evening. Fresh pineapple chunks absorb the flavor of the tequila, while fragrant stalks of lemon grass, mint sprigs, and slices of lemon and lime lend an Oriental mystique. Jamaican-style ginger ale added just prior to serving gives sparkle to this intriguing drink. Even after the punch is gone, guests enthusiastically munch on the fruit and spice.

2 large ripe pineapples, cut into chunks
1 liter of silver tequila
4–6 fresh stalks of lemon grass with rough outer leaves removed, cut in half lengthwise, then cut into 2-inch segments and slightly mashed to release flavor
2 cans (46 ounces each) pineapple juice
1 cup freshly squeezed lemon juice
2 lemons, sliced
3 limes, sliced
½ cup freshly squeezed lime juice
2 bunches fresh mint, lemon verbena, lemon balm, or a combination
ginger syrup or simple syrup (optional; page 42)
2–3 twelve-ounce bottles Reed's Original Ginger Brew
garnishes: lime slices, chunks of fresh unpeeled pineapple, fresh mint sprigs

Place the pineapple chunks in a 2-gallon glass jar and cover with the tequila. Add the lemon grass segments, pineapple and lemon juices, and add the lemon slices and chill several hours or overnight. A few hours prior to serving, add the lime slices and lime juice, the fresh herb sprigs, and ginger syrup or simple syrup to taste if desired. Just before serving, top mixture with ginger ale and ladle into tall glasses with plenty of ice and pineapple chunks. Garnish and serve.

Serves 20 or more

Piñata Ponche
(Lucinda's Festive Holiday Punch)

The colorful surprises within this enticing libation remind me of the candy treasures hidden within a Mexican piñata. Whole fresh cranberries, blueberries, kumquats, and slices of citrus and golden peaches sparkle in this ruby-red punch. The tart acidic contrast of cranberry juice and silver tequila are naturals. Further enhanced with cinnamon sticks and jamaica (dried hibiscus flowers), this holiday punch makes everyone merry.

1 package (12 ounces) fresh cranberries
1 gallon cranberry juice
1 bottle (1.75 liters) silver tequila
2 cups Cointreau
1 6-ounce can frozen limeade concentrate (optional)
4 navel oranges, sliced
1 handful jamaica (dried hibiscus blossoms)
3 10-inch cinnamon sticks
2 lemons, sliced
2 limes, sliced
12 kumquats, sliced in half lengthwise
1 package (12 ounces) frozen peaches
1 package (12 ounces) frozen blueberries
2 or 3 12-ounce bottles Reed's Original Ginger Brew (Jamaican-style ginger ale)
2–3 star fruit, sliced

Several days in advance, rinse the cranberries and drain in a colander; freeze them on a tray, then store in a freezer bag. Use half of them to freeze in decorative ice cubes, one per cube. Pour the cranberry juice, tequila, Cointreau, and limeade concentrate into a 2½-gallon container; add the sliced oranges, jamaica flowers, and cinnamon sticks; chill overnight. A few hours before serving, add remaining sliced citrus and frozen peaches. Just prior to serving, add the remaining frozen cranberries, the blueberries, star fruit, and ginger ale to taste. Serve in long-stemmed wine glasses filled with the decorative cranberry ice cubes and slices of star fruit.

Note: You can also add a strip of orange peel to each ice cube before freezing.

Serves 30 or more.

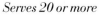

Ponche en Atotonilco

A boisterous street party takes place every night from November 30 to December 8 in the tequila-producing town of Atotonilco, Jalisco. One would never expect this after the sacredness of the early dawn. Each morning at 5:30 during this time, villagers carry a carved wooden virgin, *La Imaculada Concepción de María Purísima*, through the streets on their shoulders so that she will bless their homes. I joined the procession from the *iglesia* (church) in the plaza down a long cobblestone street packed with devoted followers, who sang and prayed to their patron saint.

That night, the solemnity of the chilly dawn was magically transformed into fiesta and revelry. The streets that had been blessed by the Virgin that morning hosted the evening's *posada*, a festivity that welcomes people door to door. Neighbors had worked for months in an effort to make their street the most impressive. They had strung intricate paper cutouts, banners, flags, and colorful crepe-paper flowers across the streets and had gaily adorned the doorways and street lamps. Firecrackers exploded in the sky, church bells clanged, and small bands playing *tambores* (drums) resonated. Troupes of animated dancers dressed in costumes of *muertos* (skeletons), *diablos* (devils), and wild animals performed in the streets.

On each corner, vendors sold crispy *buñelos* (crullers) drizzled with a syrup of *piloncillo*, *churros* (twisted fritters sprinkled with cinnamon sugar), and *cajeta* candies made from sweetened goat's milk. Children sucked the nectar from sugar-cane segments and munched on roasted *cacahuates* and *palomitas* (peanuts and popcorn). Others ate steamed garbanzos tucked into small brown paper sacks and sprinkled with fresh lime juice, salt, and chile powder.

Dense crowds paraded through the streets. Merrymakers knocked on the doors of houses, welcomed by women offering trays of simmering *ponche*, thick and flavorful concoctions brimming with fruits—guayaba, granada, tamarindo, jamaica—spiced with cinnamon and sprinkled with crushed pecans. Each ponche was a specialty of the house, some of great renown, as the lines forming outside that home attested. Gallon jugs filled with tequila from one of the town's three distilleries was plentiful, and some revelers used it to spike the punch.

I saw a group of mariachis in obsidian-colored suits studded with shiny silver buttons and bearing the words *Tequila El Viejito* blazingly embroidered across their backs. Introducing myself as an *amiga* of the owner of the distillery, I found myself with attentive chaperons, although some of the town's matrons looked on with disdain at a gringa following the mariachis. One man hired the mariachis for hours to serenade his family and neighbors. Everyone was imbibing tequila-laden ponche and singing passionately from their chairs parked in the street in front of the house. But at the stroke of midnight, the lead mariachi banished me to my hotel where, he said, "nice girls must be in at that hour." I admit that I longed for the freedom to sing and dance and drink tequila in the streets until dawn. *¡Gringa en Mexico con corazón mexicana!*

Ponche de Posada

For fiestas and posadas during the holidays, Mexicans imbibe steaming cups of punches laced with tequila and tropical fruits from small earthenware *jarros*. I always have a huge pot simmering on my stove on Christmas morning, filling my whole house with its luscious and welcoming aroma. Sometimes this punch is hard to duplicate in the United States because of the unavailability of the exotic fruits. However, many markets north of the border, especially the Mexican *pulgas* (flea markets) carry them during the Christmas season especially for the ponche.

I have allowed for some substitutions in my version and have found that tropical fruit nectars add flavor when the fresh fruits are not available. Oriental markets are often a good source for lemon grass and *tamarindo* (tamarind pods), whose tart, sticky pulp gives a unique flavor.

1 sugar cane stalk approximately 4 feet long, cut into segments

3 quarts water

6 stalks lemon grass, rough outer leaves removed, cut into 3-inch pieces, slightly mashed (optional)

1 pound *tejocote* (small, round yellow fruit popular in Mexico for punches), or crab apples, or assorted dried fruits

1 cup golden raisins

1 pound *piloncillo* or brown sugar

1 *membrillo* (quince), about ¾ pound or 2 crisp Asian pears, cut into wedges

1 pound *guayaba* (guava), quartered, or assorted mixed dried fruits

5 tamarindo pods, peeled

1 cup jamaica (dried hibiscus flowers)

3 Granny Smith apples, sliced

6 sticks cinnamon, each 3 inches long

1 teaspoon whole allspice

¼ teaspoon whole cloves

1 lemon, sliced

2 quarts fruit nectar (such as guava, guanabana, or apricot)

2 oranges, sliced

1 lemon, sliced

1 liter (or more) of your favorite tequila

With a sharp, sturdy knife, trim away the tough peel of the sugar cane segments; cut each segment into lengthwise quarters. Place the water in a large stockpot along with the lemon grass, tejocote, dried fruits, raisins, and half of the piloncillo. Bring to boil, then reduce heat and simmer for 20 minutes. Add the membillo (or pears), guavas, tamarindos, jamaica, apples, and spices along with the fruit nectar, sweetening with the remaining piloncillo to taste, and simmer for about an hour until slightly thickened and aromatic. Add the sliced citrus during the last 15 minutes. Ladle piping hot into mugs, allowing guests to add tequila to taste.

Serves 20

hand painted nopal cactus mugs from Dolores Hidalgo, Guanajuato, Mexico

TEQUILA WHIMSIES

*¡Arriba
abajo
por centro
a dentro!*

*Up
down
to the middle
and down the hatch!*

Gimmicks for selling tequila abound. I've seen barmaids hand out shot glasses instead of bullets from leather *bandoleras* slung across their shoulders, then fill the shot glasses from a bottle of tequila pulled out of a gun holster. Bars across the country, especially those catering to college crowds, devise sophomoric ways to peddle tequila, from Jello shots to "slammers."

Slammers

Years ago, I asked a group of flirtatious young Mexican waiters to surprise me with a special tequila drink. I should have thought twice. They soon came to the table, *hechando gritos* (yelling) to distract me, while one waiter sneaked up behind me. He slammed a glass covered with a napkin down on the table, quickly tipped my head back and poured something sweet and foamy but strong down my throat. "Muppet," they answered when I asked them what I had imbibed—mostly tequila with a splash of Seven-Up.

Before I could resist, it happened again. This time, someone placed a thick folded napkin upon my head, whacking the shot glass upon it. *"¡Coscorrón!"* they chuckled as I was forced once again to swallow. This time, it was tequila mixed with beer. In Spanish, a *coscorrón* is a blow to the head, and a few of these shots will certainly do it! I will stick to sipping my tequila slowly, *gracias*.

Cascada (waterfall)

Now this one is more my style. Pick up a shot glass filled with beer and hold it between your thumb and index finger. Using the same hand, place a shot of tequila between the index finger and the middle finger, and another shot of beer between your middle and ring finger. I hope you will be more coordinated than I when attempting this feat, letting the tequila cascade into your mouth along with the beer—instead of inhaling it!

Submarino

Beer has always been a favorite chaser for shots of tequila, but this one combines the two in one glass. Fill a shot glass with silver tequila. Invert a whisky tumbler over it, pressing the shot glass to its bottom as you quickly flip it over. Slowly fill the whisky tumbler with cold beer. The tequila drizzles out as it is sipped, but macho men, apparently unable to wait, down it in one long gulp.

Less maneuvering is necessary for another nautical version, the Boilermaker: simply sink a shot glass filled with tequila into a mug of Mexican beer. *¡Hasta el fondo!* (To the bottom of the glass!)

The French Shot

This drink requires (or perhaps creates) intimate partners, as it is a rather lascivious way to drink tequila, no doubt about it. The most difficult part is deciding who gets to drink the first shot of tequila.

Have an icy shot of tequila readily available. Face each other. Your partner holds a lime wedge between his\her teeth, succulent side out. You lick your companion's neck, then sprinkle the spot with salt. Lick the salt, shoot the tequila, then bite into the lime. Reverse roles—or change partners. Ooh la la!

Oyster Shooters

Oysters and shots of tequila may have something in common: passionate consumers! And you usually want more than one.

Per serving:

1 medium-sized fresh raw oyster
1 tablespoon salsa mexicana or sangrita (page 57)
2 splashes Tabasco
Juice of ½ lime
Salt to taste

Place a medium-sized raw oyster in a shot glass. Top it with salsa, Tabasco, lime juice, and salt. Fill remainder of shot glass with tequila. Slurp and sigh!

Note: For a Pacific rim version (the Japanese are great tequila fans) top the oyster with minced, pickled ginger, a pinch of wasabi, and sprinkle with salmon roe and a splash of soy.

Serves 1

sprig of
chile pequín

ELEGANT AFTER-DINNER DRINKS

*Con barriga llena,
el corazón contento.
La tequila buena,
las penas ya no siento.*

✺

*With a full belly,
a happy heart.
A good tequila,
my troubles depart.*

Edward Weston's memories of Mexico in the early 1920s are as sensitive and beautiful as his photographs. Said Weston, "Strange how one can understand a foreign tongue with tequila in one's belly." After imbibing these luscious after-dinner drinks, you may be speaking Spanish too!

Para Mi Amante
(For My Lover)

In Provence, the season's ripest fruits are layered with sugar and spice and covered with Armagnac to create a luscious liqueur. I use a fine tequila añejo and tropical fruits in my rendition and serve it, along with some of the fruit, in champagne glasses. It also makes a fine sauce to spoon over flan, cheesecake, ice cream, pound cake, or fresh fruit slices. Splurge for a pretty widemouthed jar to show off the colorful array of ripe raspberries, blueberries, orange and lemon slices, star fruit, mango slices, and pomegranate seeds steeped in tequila. A whole split vanilla bean and cinnamon sticks further enhance the look and flavor. Make this delectable concoction a month in advance to allow the tequila,

fruit, and spices to mellow. It makes exquisite Christmas and Valentine's Day gifts.

2 valencia or navel oranges, sliced

1 lemon, sliced

1 pint blueberries

½ pint raspberries

1 pound slightly firm mangos, peeled and cut in wedges

2 star fruit (carambola), sliced (will form star shapes)

seeds of 1 pomegranate (optional)

½ pound cherries or purple grapes (optional)

1 bottle premium tequila añejo (750 ml)

peel of 1 orange cut in continuous spiral or long strips

1 vanilla bean, split

3 cinnamon sticks

¼ cup or more simple or citrus syrup (page 42)

In a 2- or 3-quart widemouthed jar (preferably a decorative one), layer the fruits placing the more fragile fruits on the top layers. Cover with tequila, and insert cinnamon, vanilla bean, and orange peel spiral in the jar. Add syrup. Gently shake jar occasionally. Simply add more layers of fruit as they come into season and more tequila and syrup to taste as the level of this euphoric liqueur diminishes. Serve at room temperature.

Note: For gifts, this recipe may be made in small jars. For added freshness, I like to keep it refrigerated. Use organically grown citrus or any other favorite fruits.

Rompope
(Mexican Eggnog)

Early Christmas morning, friends and neighbors gather at my house to sing carols accompanied by guitar and plenty of eggnog. There's a special twist to this tradition: guests arrive wearing pajamas, and the eggnog is spiked with tequila.

Nuns in Mexican convents first made rompope, a rich thick eggnog with ingredients introduced to the New World from Spain: sugar, nutmeg, brandy, and cream. Most eggnogs are too dense and cloying for my taste, so my version, laced with tequila, is rich and luscious but not as sweet as those made with rum or brandy. It is smooth, flavored with spirals of citrus peel, and dusted with freshly grated nutmeg. Most people swear that it is the best they've ever tasted. Serve rompope in small pottery mugs or elegant crystal sherry glasses. I use Sauza's Tres Generaciones tequila in this recipe.

12 egg yolks, separated
1 pound confectioners' sugar
1 bottle (750 ml) tequila añejo
1 teaspoon Mexican vanilla extract or ½ split vanilla pod
continuous spiral of 1 orange peel (pith removed)
continuous spiral of 1 lemon peel (pith removed)
2 quarts half-and-half
garnish: 1 freshly grated nutmeg

With a whisk, beat egg yolks in a large bowl until thick and pale yellow in color; slowly add sugar and half the tequila, mixing well. Let stand for an hour, then whisk in the remaining tequila, vanilla, citrus peel, and half-and-half. Pour into a large pitcher and chill overnight. Fill each glass with eggnog, adding a piece of twisted orange peel and dust with a pinch of freshly grated nutmeg.

Serves 16

Almendrado
(Almond-Flavored Tequila Liqueur)

The Orendain family in Jalisco produces tequila as well as an almond-flavored tequila liqueur called Crema de Almendrado. When this liqueur is served in snifters, over ice with a twist of lemon, or in coffees, the flavor of tequila remains intact, making it less sweet than other almond-flavored liqueurs. Because it is hard to find, I always bring a bottle home with me when I cross the border. Its availability may improve, but it now has limited distribution in the United States. Meanwhile, my homemade version, redolent of toasted almonds and vanilla with a hint of cinnamon, makes wonderful gifts, especially when bottled in decorative jars or bottles.

For the almond/tequila mixture:
8 ounces whole unpeeled almonds, dark roasted (page 119)
½ vanilla bean, split
1 bottle (750 ml) gold tequila

For the spicy syrup:
2 or more tablespoons spicy piloncillo syrup (page 43)
¼ teaspoon pure almond extract
1 3-inch cinnamon stick

Coarsely chop the almonds. Place them in a jar, along with the vanilla bean and cinnamon stick. Cover with the tequila and steep for 2 weeks in a cool, dark place, shaking gently occasionally (a murky sediment is natural). Strain several times through paper coffee filters.

Add syrup and almond extract in small increments, tasting after each addition, until satisfied with flavor. Pour into sterilized dark-colored jars; allow to set for 2 weeks, adding more syrup if needed.

Note: The spicy syrup also makes a tasty sweetener for coffee drinks.

Makes about 3 ½ cups

Ambrosia
(Golden Nectar of the Gods)

Reminiscent of tropical fruit, this amber-colored liqueur is enhanced by the flavor of gold tequila and tropical spices—cardamom, vanilla pod, allspice, and cloves. I spoon Ambrosia over ice cream, fresh fruit, flan, or pound cake, or serve it in elegant cordial glasses. It's great after a spicy meal.

1 small orange, sliced
2½ ounces candied ginger, chopped (about ½ cup)
1 cup golden raisins
3 ounces dried mangos and/or papaya, loosely chopped
1 teaspoon whole allspice
¼ teaspoon whole cloves
1 teaspoon cardamom pods, slightly crushed
1 cinnamon stick
1 bottle (750 ml) gold tequila
2 tablespoons or more ginger syrup, citrus syrup, or simple syrup (page 42)

In a 1 ½-quart jar, layer the candied ginger, raisins, mango, and spices between the orange slices. Cover with tequila and allow to steep for 2 weeks. Sweeten to taste if desired. Store in a cool, dark place. Simply add more fruit and tequila to the starter mixture as needed. Great for gifts!

Note: Use this in a glaze or sauce for ham or pork.

Makes about a quart.

Licor de Margarita
(Margarita Liqueur)

Simple and straightforward but elegant, this liqueur is not as sweet as most. It looks inviting in the bottle, its long swirls of citrus promising refreshment. Keep it in the refrigerator and serve it straight or on the rocks with a twist of orange peel—before or after a meal. Take a bottle of this to the host of a dinner party instead of a bottle of wine.

1 bottle (750 ml) fine silver or reposado tequila

peel of 1 orange cut in a continuous spiral or long strips (without white pith)

peel of 1 lime cut in a continuous spiral or long strips (without white pith)

4–6 ounces Cointreau

Share a shot of tequila with a friend while making this. Add citrus peel to tequila remaining in the bottle, and add then Cointreau to taste. Keep refrigerated, and serve in sherry glasses. Remove citrus peel if liqueur starts to become bitter.

Note: See Dazey Stripper, in Resources.

Makes about 12 2-ounce shots

Cactus Cordial

You may have to live in Mexico (or New Mexico, Arizona, California, or Texas) to make this desert rose of a drink. Serve ice cold.

2 pounds prickly pear fruit, peeled and quartered

1 bottle (750 ml) silver tequila

1 cup citrus syrup (page 42) or 1½ cups Cointreau

Combine ingredients in a widemouth jar. Let stand in a cool, dark place for several weeks, stirring and pressing down on the fruit occasionally. Strain through a paper coffee-filter and pour into decorative jars, discarding fruit.

Makes about a quart

"Tequila en un jarro"
Tequila in an earthenware mug

CAFÉ

Coffee-Tequila Drinks

Tequila and coffee are soulmates. Strong in character, earthy and robust in flavor, they are easily paired in drinks. Whether served hot or on the rocks, laced with exotic liqueurs or with a cap of sweet cream, coffee-tequila drinks are the perfect finale for a special dinner or the start of a lazy Sunday. Serve them instead of dessert, topped with freshly whipped cream and stirred with a cinnamon stick.

After dinner, I like to set up a tray of tequilas, liqueurs, and a pot of freshly brewed coffee accompanied by bowls filled with assorted toppings and whipped cream. Let guests create their own concoctions. Transparent stemmed glasses show off these sumptuous drinks beautifully. See Resources for Mexican coffee.

Compatible Liqueurs for Tequila Drinks

★ Coffee liqueurs such as Kahlúa, St. Maarten's Café, Tía María, Coloma

★ Orange liqueurs such as Cointreau or Grand Marnier

★ Almond-flavored liqueurs such as Orendain Crema de Almendrado or Amaretto di Saronno

★ Tuaca, an Italian brandy-based liqueur

★ Licor Cuarenta y Tres (43), a Spanish brandy-based liqueur

★ Damiana, a Mexican liqueur flavored with damiana, a wild herb

Flavorings

Mexican Vanilla

Vanilla—heady and redolent of musky earth and flowers—is a natural for coffee-tequila drinks. When I brew coffee, I usually add a teaspoon of vanilla to the pot. Few people realize that the vanilla bean is the dried pod of a tropical orchid. I have seen the green pods hanging from a climbing vine (*Vanilla planifolia*) in the Papantla region of Veracruz. The unripened pods must first ferment and dry before they produce the pure, exquisite essence of vanilla. Look for bottled pure Mexican vanilla extract in Latin American markets—or bring some home with you the next time you cross the border.

Mexican Whipped Cream

½ pint whipping cream
confectioners' sugar to taste (2–3 tablespoons)
¼ teaspoon Mexican vanilla extract
1 tablespoon tequila añejo

In a chilled stainless-steel mixing bowl with chilled beaters, whip cream until it thickens slightly. Slowly add confectioners' sugar, vanilla, and tequila añejo, and beat until it forms stiff mounds.

Spicy Piloncillo Syrup

Especially for coffee drinks, make a rich dark-brown syrup from *piloncillo* (Mexican unrefined cone sugar), cinnamon, and clove. It dissolves easily in coffee, imparting a smooth texture. (See page 43.)

Café Atotonilco

The tequila-producing town of Atotonilco, Jalisco, with its narrow cobblestone streets and colonial churches, reminds me more of Spain than of Mexico. The townspeople justifiably boast of the coffee made there, and sipping it during the siesta hours is a daily ritual for some residents.

The open-air shop renowned for its *café estilo atotonilco* also hosts daily domino games, where men (and men only) hold small glasses filled with the strong dark libation, pensively contemplating their next move. I braved the curious stares of the patrons in order to sample that much-touted brew.

The sullen coffee-master seemed none too eager to welcome a woman, much less to offer me a glass, but I boldly persisted. I learned that he makes a potent coffee extract, using a slow-drip cold-water process. His dark-roasted blend of ground beans are steeped overnight, slowly dripping through tiny holes in a metal filter. Each morning, he bottles this extract to sell and to serve in his shop.

He handed me my coffee, along with a bowl of unrefined sugar that I added sparingly, although *Mexicanos* seem to add it by spoonfuls. It was indeed delicious—rich and strong. Immediately I imagined it spiked with tequila añejo and sweetened slightly with brown sugar or a splash of almond-flavored tequila. And on that hot and dusty day, I also longed to taste it on the rocks.

Fortunately, the producers of Patrón Tequila, which is distilled in Atotonilco, had the same idea. They created St. Maarten Café, a 70-proof liqueur that captures the natural essence of coffee in a fine añejo tequila. Unlike most overly sweet coffee liqueurs, St. Maarten Café stands alone perfectly well in a snifter or a shot glass, on the rocks, or in a cup of freshly brewed coffee. Its elegant packaging, a smoke-colored bottle etched with gold lettering, promises no disappointment.

Note: Coffee brewed using the cold-water process retains the rich coffee flavor without bitterness or acidity. In this concentrated form, it may be mixed with cold or boiling water to desired strength (approximately 1 part coffee to 2 or 3 parts water), making a convenient companion for parties and traveling. Cold-water drip coffee makers are available for making coffee extracts in glass beakers with filter attachments. See Resources.

Café Campestre

Atotonilco, Jalisco, is known for its tequila and its coffee alike. I had a wonderful meal with Antonio Nuñez, the owner of the distillery that produces El Viejito Tequila, at Restaurant Campestre. Afterwards, the bartender agreed to prepare us a drink that I had in mind. He rimmed a fluted glass with grated piloncillo (brown sugar will do in a pinch), poured in the famous coffee extract, and gave it some kick with locally produced El Viejito Añejo and a splash of amaretto over cracked ice. Yum!

Because it is so potent and packed with flavor, some may wish to tame Café Campestre with a layer of cream carefully poured over the back of a teaspoon. Orendain's Crema de Almendrado, when available, or homemade almendrado liqueur (page 101), less sweet than amaretto, keep the flavor of tequila prominent. Experiment with other liqueurs as well.

small saucer of grated piloncillo, brown sugar, or turbinado sugar (page 44)
¼ cup coffee extract (preferably cold-water process) or espresso, room temperature
1 ounce tequila añejo
½ ounce amaretto or 1 ounce Orendain's Crema de Almendrado or homemade almendrado (page 101)
cracked ice
additional sugar for sweetening (optional)
cream (optional)
cinnamon stick for stirring

Dip the rim of a stemmed glass in a saucer of tequila, then twirl lightly in the piloncillo. Pour in coffee, tequila, and liqueur; carefully add cracked ice. Sprinkle with additional piloncillo and stir with a cinnamon stick.

Note: Omit the almond liqueur, add ½ ounce more tequila, and sweeten with spicy syrup (page 103) to taste.

Serves 1

St. Maarten Café Shooter

Rambunctious and robust, this coffee-tequila combination will certainly wake you up!

¾ ounce Patrón Silver Tequila
¾ ounce St. Maarten Café

Swirl ingredients together in a small snifter. Enjoy!

Serves 1

Ruso Negro
(Black Russian)

The spirited flavor of tequila gives vodka some competition in the after-dinner favorite.

1½ ounces silver tequila
½ ounce your favorite coffee liqueur (see page 103)
ice cubes
garnish: twist of lemon peel and two whole coffee beans

Mix the tequila and coffee liqueur and serve on the rocks with the lemon peel and coffee beans.

Serves 1

Café de Cajeta
(Coffee Flavored with Mexican Caramel)

Cajeta is a rich, luscious caramel sauce, something like a thick butterscotch made from goat's milk. The Konditori, a popular restaurant founded by a Danish family in Mexico City's Zona Rosa, serves it in cappuccino dusted with cinnamon.

1 cup of freshly brewed cappuccino, made with a full-bodied coffee
dollop of Mexican cajeta
cinnamon

Place a dollop of cajeta in a mug and fill with steaming cappuccino, dust with cinnamon, and serve.

Note: Cajeta is available in glass jars in Mexican specialty stores.

Serves 1

Café Caramba
(Frosty Mexican Cappuccino)

Dessert in a glass! This drink is frothy, fabulous, and deliciously decadent.

1½ cups strong coffee, preferably made from cold-water process, room temperature
6 ounces tequila añejo
2 ounces coffee liqueur
2 ounces almendrado (page 101)
½ teaspoon ground cinnamon
¼ teaspoon Mexican vanilla extract
1 pint vanilla bean or coffee ice cream
cinnamon sticks for stirring

Combine all ingredients except ice cream in a blender pitcher and refrigerate. Just prior to serving, add ice cream and whirl in the blender. Pour over ice into long-stemmed glasses or champagne flutes. Dust lightly with cinnamon, stir with a cinnamon stick, and serve immediately.

Note: Omit the almendrado, double the coffee liqueur, or use 3 ounces coffee liqueur plus 1 tablespoon amaretto. Experiment with other liqueurs as well.

Serves 6

FESTIVE WAYS TO SERVE COFFEE AND OTHER AFTER-DINNER DRINKS

Lightly dip the rim of the coffee mug or stemmed glass in a shallow bowl of beaten egg whites, tequila, or liqueur, then twirl the rim of the glass in any of the following: cinnamon sugar, turbinado sugar, coarse white sparkling sugar crystals, grated piloncillo or brown sugar, grated Mexican chocolate, or finely ground coffee beans.

Use the following for toppings:

▼ Sweet cream or half-and-half
▼ Mexican Whipped Cream (page 103)
▼ Sparkling colored sugar crystals
▼ Chocolate-covered coffee beans
▼ Twist of orange or lemon peel
▼ Crumbled hard candies such as English toffee, butterscotch, or cinnamon
▼ Toasted and ground almonds
▼ Cinnamon sticks as stirrers
▼ Freshly grated nutmeg
▼ Powdered cinnamon
▼ Spiral of orange or lemon peel
▼ Candied orange peel
▼ Grated Mexican chocolate

Adiós

After dinner, tequila and coffee are perfect compadres. Add a mellow and flavorful liqueur and you have a happy trio. By tasting, you can decide on the proportion of tequila to liqueur. Experimenting to find your favorite combinations and toppings is part of the fun and a memorable *adiós* to the evening.

Warm mugs or stemmed glasses by rinsing them in hot water. Choose one of the frosted rims from page 105; add about ⅔ cup freshly brewed coffee, top with a shot of gold or añejo tequila and your favorite liqueur, and garnish. Mexican Whipped Cream and sugar or Spicy Piloncillo Syrup are optional. The following are six of my favorite combinations; try them as well in cappuccino, decreasing the ingredients proportionally. For other liqueur and garnish suggestions see page 38.

Naranja Dulce
(Sweet Orange)

freshly brewed strong coffee

1½ ounces tequila añejo

¾ ounces Cointreau

Mexican Whipping Cream, page 103 (optional)

garnish: grated Mexican chocolate to rim glass and sprinkle on top of each drink; spiral of orange peel

Piel Canela
(Cinnamon Skin)

freshly brewed strong coffee

1½ ounce tequila añejo

1 ounce Tuaca liqueur

Mexican Whipping Cream, optional

garnishes: cinnamon sugar to rim glass and sprinkle on each drink; cinnamon stick for stirring

Bésame Mucho
(Kiss Me Often)

freshly brewed strong coffee

1½ ounces tequila añejo

¾ ounce Damiana liqueur or Licor 43

Mexican Whipping Cream (optional)

garnishes: orange twist and freshly grated nutmeg and sugar to rim glass; candied orange spiral; cinnamon stick for stirring

Café Olé

freshly brewed strong coffee

1½ ounces tequila añejo

1 ounce Tía Maria, Kahlúa, or Coloma

Mexican Whipping Cream (optional)

garnishes: finely ground coffee beans and sugar to rim glass; chocolate covered coffee beans; cinnamon stick for stirring

México Lindo

freshly brewed strong coffee

1½ ounces tequila añejo

½ ounce amaretto or ¾ ounce almendrado

Mexican Whipping Cream (optional)

garnishes: turbinado or brown sugar to rim glass sprinkling of toasted ground almonds

St. Maarten Café
"Tex Mex"

Remember, St. Maarten Café liqueur already has tequila in it!

freshly brewed hot coffee

¾ ounce St. Maarten Café liqueur

¾ ounce Patrón Añejo tequila

Mexican Whipping Cream, optional

garnishes: freshly grated nutmeg and brown sugar to rim coffee mug; chocolate shavings or chocolate-covered coffee bean

Café del Diablo
(Devil's Coffee)

The renowned Café Brûlot of New Orleans travels south of the border in my version—a devilishly good drink—with añejo tequila instead of brandy. Turn off the lights and enjoy the spectacle of this flambéed treat.

2 tablespoons brown sugar

peel of 1 orange, cut in a continuous spiral (without pith)

peel of 1 lemon, cut in a continuous spiral (without pith)

12 whole cloves

2 sticks of cinnamon, broken into bits

¾ cup tequila añejo

3 cardamom pods, slightly bruised with the back of a knife (optional)

2 tablespoons Cointreau

4 cups hot strong coffee

In a chafing dish or a fireproof dish over an open flame, combine sugar, citrus peel, spices, and tequila. Heat, stirring gently with a ladle, but do not boil. Place some tequila in a tablespoon with some brown sugar, and light it. Ceremoniously (but cautiously), use it to ignite the simmering contents. Stir gently for a minute, allowing the flambéeing liquid to cascade from the ladle. Gradually pour in the hot coffee from the side of the dish, so as not to extinguish the flames, stirring for another minute. Immediately ladle into demitasse cups and serve.

Serves 6

After-dinner Tequila/Liqueur Coolers

Although a fine añejo tequila swirled in a snifter makes a perfect nightcap anytime, I sometimes enjoy tequila mixed with a favorite liqueur on the rocks. During warm weather, after-dinner drinks served over ice can take the place of a rich dessert. I am not a fan of overly sweet drinks with a lot of ingredients. I keep my after-dinner drinks simple so that the flavor of the tequila remains intact.

Pour your favorite tequila and after-dinner liqueur over ice in a highball glass, stirring gently. Garnish with a twist of citrus. You may wish to cap it with a layer of cream poured over the back of a spoon and dusted with freshly grated nutmeg or cinnamon. Use any of the suggested garnishes on page 105. The following are a few of my special-occasion favorites.

Pancho Villa

Game fish mounted on the walls seem to be swimming amid sun-burned gringo fishermen at Bobby and Chacha van Wormer's Playa de Cortéz fishing hotel in Baja, California del Sur, Mexico. Some say it's the best fishing in Baja. The bartender, Hector Castro Ruíz, told me many tales as he made his specialty drink. Laced with Baja's renowned liqueur, Damiana, it is reputed to have aphrodisiac powers.

twist of lime peel
1¾ ounces Sauza Conmemorativo tequila
½ ounces Damiana liqueur
cracked ice
garnish: pinch of freshly grated nutmeg

Rim highball glass with twist of lime peel. Pour the tequila and Damiana over ice, drop in the lime peel, and sprinkle lightly with the nutmeg. *¡Cuidado!*

Serves 1

Aguanta la Güera
(Resist the Blonde)

Light and golden, this drink is like a sparkle of sunshine. Its name is a play on words in Spanish because it rhymes with the title of a popular song "Guantanamera." The mere utterance of the phrase "Aguanta la güera" always gives Mexicans a big laugh. Loosely translated, it means, "Back off from the blonde, Buster."

twist of orange peel
1½ ounces fine silver tequila
½ ounce Cointreau or Licor 43
Cracked ice

Rub the rim of a highball glass with a twist of orange. Mix together the tequila and the Cointreau over ice, and serve.

Serves 1

Medias de Seda
(Silk Stockings)

This is a favorite after-dinner drink of Mexican women. It is luxurious, smooth as silk, pretty, and pink. Pablo Cordero, bartender for the Camarena de Tequila (Tequila Chamber of Commerce), a man with an uncanny resemblance to Diego Rivera, made this for me in Guadalajara. He proudly displayed his bartending skills—and Mexico's spirit—in Paris in 1978, when he mixed tequila drinks at an international spirits convention.

1½ ounces silver tequila
2 ounces evaporated milk
1 ounce Crema de Cacao
½ ounce grenadine syrup
½ cup cracked ice
garnish: ground cinnamon for rim of glass

Mix ingredients together in a blender with the ice until creamy. Pour into long-stemmed cocktail glass dusted with cinnamon.

Serves 1

Amor de Montezuma
(Emperor's Love)

The Aztec emperor Montezuma voraciously consumed a chocolate beverage laced with fragrant flowers, chile peppers, and spice. The only ingredient missing was tequila! Maidens served Montezuma his chocolate unheated and unsweetened. My version is more contemporary in its flavorings, sure to bring Mexico to your hearthside on a cold wintery night.

1½ ounces tequila, gold or añejo
1 ounce liqueur (Almendrado, Cointreau, or Tía Maria)
⅛ teaspoon each vanilla and almond extract (optional)
1 cup Mexican hot chocolate, prepared
garnish: ground cinnamon to rim mug or cup

Mix the tequila, liqueur, and almond extract in a mug or cup; add prepared hot chocolate and serve.

Note: Look for Mexican chocolate, flavored with cinnamon and ground almonds, in Mexican specialty shops. My favorite is Ibarra (follow directions on the box to prepare).

Serves 1

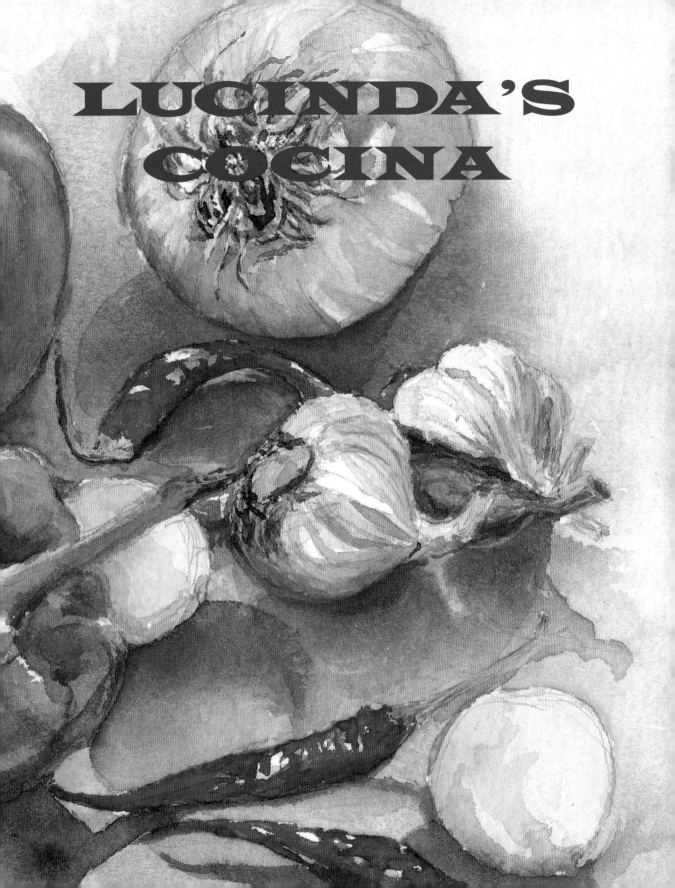

LUCINDA'S COCINA

COOKING WITH TEQUILA

*Tomas tequila
quema la gallina*

✳

*Too many shots
spoils the cook.*

To match tequila's spirit, I have created fiesta recipes filled with color, flavor, and surprise. Their unexpected ingredients and eye-catching presentations promise festivity and fun. Many of these recipes are quite versatile: a single recipe can be combined with several others. (After all, one good thing leads to another!) Although some of these recipes list many ingredients and have several steps, they are not difficult to prepare, and the end result is delicious food that you will not find at other parties. Most of the dishes may be made in advance and lend themselves to buffet fare to simplify entertaining. Of course, they are designed with tequila drinks in mind.

Surprisingly, Mexicans rarely cook with tequila, but that country has inspired much of my cooking. From Mexico's kitchen, I have gathered ingredients and techniques; from her garden, herbs and chiles; and from her cantina, tequila. Tequila aficionados are most likely as passionate about chiles, garlic, spices, and other lusty flavors as I am. My recipes reflect this fervor—spirited and lively food for spirited and lively people: fiesta fare!

"You *cook* with tequila?" people ask me, rather astonished. They assume that tequila's robust and assertive flavor belongs in a rowdy cantina instead of in the cocina. But tequila is not just for drinking! Its lively flavor paired with fresh and delicious ingredients lends new dimensions and creativity to cooking. In fact, tequila seems to enhance many dishes, often in a pleasingly subtle fashion.

Instead of overwhelming with bravado, it simply balances and brings out natural flavors. Tequila can be used in uncooked foods—salsas, marinades, soups, and salads—or in cooking. When you flambé, sauté, or simmer, the alcohol burns off, leaving the sweet and mellow fruitiness of the agave.

Tequila mellows the acidity of fresh lime juice and other citrus. Its earthy and robust nature is a perfect partner for frijoles and pungent dried red chiles, garlic, and spices. And its innate peppery flavor highlights fresh vegetables, herbs, and tropical fruits. Tequila's versatility makes it at home in a searing chile salsa as well as in an elegant flan custard.

Experiment with silver, gold, reposado, or añejo tequilas in the following recipes, as well as with tequilas infused with fresh herbs, chile peppers, or fruits.

Dried Spices

Freshly ground spices make all the difference in a dish and are important ingredients in many of these recipes. Purchase whole spices in small quantities to grind as needed in a small electric coffee/spice grinder or volcanic stone *molcajete*. The flavor far surpasses that of purchased ground spices/chiles. Keep on hand whole spices such as peppercorns (black, white, and a colorful mélange), coriander seeds, cumin seeds, and cloves for grinding, as well as nutmeg for grating. Cinnamon sticks and vanilla pods are handy staples as well.

Chiles

Dried and fresh chiles are essential to many of the following dishes. There are no substitutes for their unique flavor. These recipes call for chiles that are readily available in North American markets or by mail order (see Resources).

Dried chiles

★ **Chile Colorado:** New Mexico red chiles traditionally hung in *ristras* (clusters) to dry in the sun; popular in northern Mexican and Southwestern cuisines; 5-7 inches long with a bright, earthy flavor ranging from mild to *picoso* (hot).

★ **Chile de Árbol:** 2-3 inches long; shiny, bright red, thin skin and lots of seeds; searing hot; adds instant flavor to a dish when freshly ground and sprinkled on it, or toasted and ground into a sauce; cayenne or *japón* may be substituted.

★ **Chipotle:** Dried, ripened smoked jalapeño; toasty brown and wrinkly; smoke-and-fire flavored; often canned in *adobo*, a thick sauce flavored with tomatoes, vinegar, and spices.

★ **Pequín *(Chilpiquín)*:** Tiny, oval-shaped, and fiery hot; used interchangeably with the small round *tepín* (*chiltepín*) for sangrita and salsas.

★ **Ancho:** Dried poblano 4-5 inches long; thick-fleshed and wrinkly with piquant, raisiny flavor.

★ **Guajillo:** 4-6 inches long; shiny and thin-skinned; sweet-hot flavor; may be used interchangeably with the *puya*.

★ **Puya:** 3-4 inches long; has a curved tip and is thin-fleshed; slightly acidic with a fiery finish; guajillo or árbol may be substituted.

Fresh Chiles

★ **New Mexico or Anaheim (green or red-ripened)**: 6-8 inches long; thin-skinned with flavor ranging from mild to picoso; to use, roast and peel.

★ **Poblano**: 4-5 inches long; dark green, thick-fleshed, triangular, and wrinkly; flavor that ranges from sweet and mild to fiery; to use, roast and peel.

★ **Jalapeño**: 2-3 inches long; bright green ripening to red; thick-fleshed and shiny; heat ranges from mild to hot.

★ **Serrano**: 1-2 inches long; dark green ripening to red; usually very hot with a fresh, bright flavor.

★ **Habanero**: 1½-2 inches long; wrinkly, bright orange ripening to red; fruity but ferociously hot.

★ **Fresno**: Resembles a ripened red jalapeño but usually hotter.

Quesos

Mexican-style cheeses are becoming more readily available in North American markets but often lack the flavor and texture of those produced in Mexico. Taste before using. See Resources for mail-order sources.

★ *Asadero*: This cheese is a specialty of northern Mexico. It is a soft, white cheese that melts perfectly for *chile con queso* and *queso flameado* with a flavor reminiscent of mozzarella (a combination of Monterey Jack, Muenster, or mozzarella may be substituted).

★ *Queso Blanco*: *Queso blanco*, like *asadero* and *queso Chihuahua*, is becoming more readily available in North American markets. Some cheeses labeled *queso blanco* seem virtually tasteless, however, and some are rubbery in texture. Insist on sampling before purchasing, or substitute Monterey Jack or Muenster.

★ *Queso Chihuahua*: This creamy white cheese was originally made by Mennonite communities in the northern Mexican state of Chihuahua. Today the Mennonites have dispersed, and good Chihuahua cheese is hard to find. A combination of Jack, Muenster, and mozzarella may be substituted.

ROASTING GREEN CHILES AND MAKING RAJAS

New Mexico, Anaheim, and poblano chile peppers must be roasted to remove the tough skin and to give flavor. Poke them with a fork to prevent bursting, then place them on a baking sheet. Roast 4–6 inches from the flame of a preheated broiler or char over the open flame of a grill or on a hot comal; turn occasionally for even blistering and charring.

Place in a damp dish towel or plastic bag after roasting and allow to steam for 10 minutes. The charred skin will easily peel off; do not rinse under running water or you will lose flavor.

Strips of roasted peppers are called *rajas*. Note that red or green bell peppers may be roasted in the same way. To make, simply remove seeds and stems from the roasted chiles and cut them into narrow three-inch long strips. Toss with minced garlic for added flavor.

Mermaid Feast
painted by my godson's
father, Esteban Basilio Nolasco
Ocumicho, Michoacán

"Fiesta de Las Sirenas"
Ladies Night Out

Fiesta Foods

Tostada Compuesta Fiesta

A *tostada compuesta* (layered tostada) fiesta is a fun way to entertain buffet-style. Tostadas are whole corn tortillas or tortilla wedges that have been fried in hot oil until crisp. Guests may layer them by choosing from a variety of options. Traditional choices include: refried beans (pinto or black), guacamole, crumbled or grated cheese, shredded chicken or meat, chopped tomatoes, shredded cabbage or lettuce, and salsa picante.

Recipes in this book that are good for tostadas include: Salpicón (page 140), a shredded marinated beef specialty from Northern Mexico; Pollo Enchilado (page 140), roasted chicken smothered in a chile sauce; Queso Flameado (page 120), sizzling melted cheese; Frijoles Negros Refritos (page 130), a tasty black bean dip; and Pescado Margarita (page 141), grilled fish with a spicy-citrus rub. Serve several bowls of tasty salsas, which guests may spoon over their tostadas to add color, texture, and flavor. Fiesta Margarita (page 74), in a pitcher, or Cazuela Guadalajara (page 94), a refreshing tequila fruit punch, are ideal fiesta libations. All of these dishes may be made ahead of time so that you can enjoy your own party.

Homemade tostadas

Homemade tostadas taste much fresher and crisper than most commercially available ones. With a sharp knife, cut corn tortillas into 6 triangular wedges. Heat about ½ inch of vegetable oil in a heavy skillet; add the tortilla wedges a few at a time and fry, turning occasionally, until crisp and golden (about 3 minutes). Remove with a slotted spoon and drain on paper towels; sprinkle with salt if desired.

Fried whole corn tortillas (flour tortillas may also be used) provide a crisp, flat surface for layering fiesta foods. Using tongs, place the corn tortilla in ½ inch of hot vegetable oil and fry until crisp, turning once. Drain on paper towels.

Store tostadas in a cool place in an airtight container for up to 3 days. Reheat in a preheated 300°F oven for a few minutes before serving.

Quesos y Chile Pestos

Sizzling melted cheese with *rajas de poblano* (strips of roasted poblano peppers) is served from shallow earthenware dishes in Jalisco restaurants. The *queso* is scooped into hot flour tortillas, accompanied by grilled meats, shots of tequila, and sangrita. In Mexican restaurants in the United States, people dunk tostada chips into *chile con queso* between sips from icy margaritas. Few people, however, think of teaming tequila and cheese together in a dish, even though they are natural companions. The flavor of cheese is greatly enhanced by tequila's robust and peppery nature.

Chilled layered cheese *tortas* (terrines), flavored with fresh herbs and chiles and spiked with tequila, have become my signature dish. Filling and flavorful, cheese tortas are naturals with tequila drinks. Overlapping slices of provolone form a shell and separate colorful layers of spicy pesto and cheese fillings, which are shown off when sliced. Inspired by the traditional Italian green and garlicky basil pesto, I have ground chiles and garlic, toasted nuts and seeds, zesty herbs and freshly grated Parmesan into pestos with a decidedly Mexican flair. These flavorful pestos give character to the cheese tortas and can also be used as a condiment in marinades and sauces.

A cheese torta may be prepared several days before serving, making entertaining easy because the torta requires only last-minute garnishing. It will be the hit of your party, where your guests can slather it on crisp croutons (see page 137) or tostada chips. Serve the torta on a platter, surrounded by sprigs of fresh herbs and small fresh chile peppers and bowls of colorful salsas.

Queso Sabroso

(Zesty Goat Cheese Appetizer)

The assertive flavors of goat cheese and tequila seem to mellow each other as complementary partners in this versatile recipe. You may form Queso Sabroso into one large ball or many small round balls (called *redonditas*) and roll in freshly minced herbs, crushed dried red chile, toasted cumin seeds, or coarsely ground tostada chips. Serve with croutons or tostada chips, or use as a side dish to soups or salads.

8 ounces cream cheese, softened
4 ounces mild goat cheese
2 teaspoons olive oil
2–3 cloves garlic, minced
1 tablespoon tequila reposado (part pepper-flavored, if desired)
¼ teaspoon salt
¼ teaspoon crushed dried chile de árbol
garnishes: minced fresh herbs such as rosemary, basil, oregano, sage, epazote (press whole leaves into cheese ball); crushed and dried red chiles such as chile de árbol, cayenne, or ancho; toasted cumin seeds; or finely ground tostada chips

In a medium-sized bowl, blend the cheeses, olive oil, garlic, tequila, salt, and chile with an electric mixer; cover and refrigerate overnight. Roll into redonditas (walnut-sized balls) or form into one round cheeseball. Chill until ready to serve; just before serving, roll in the garnish of your choice.

Note: When I serve Queso Sabroso formed into one large cheeseball, I accompany it with bowls of colorful salsas.

Redonditas may be slightly flattened and coated with coarsely ground tostada chips, then broiled for 1 minute—watch carefully! Serve them on croutons as an accompaniment to salads.

Makes about 26 redonditas or one large cheeseball, or enough filling for one cheese torta.

VIVA NUEVO MEXICO VINAIGRETTE (OR MARINADE)

Green and garlicky and fragrant with fresh herbs and roasted chiles, this makes a flavorful salad dressing (try it on avocado halves!) or marinade for fish, shrimp, or chicken, or it may be drizzled over sauteed or grilled vegetables. In a small bowl, mix together 3 tablespoons Roasted Green Chile and Pecan Pesto (see page 118), 2 tablespoons white wine vinegar, 1 tablespoon fresh lime juice, and 1 tablespoon tequila reposado; slowly whisk in 1 or 2 tablespoons of olive oil. Add salt and ground pepper to taste. Makes ½ cup.

Si Pica
(Smoky Chipotle and Toasted Pepita Pesto)

This pesto is *muy picoso*—full of fire and flavor: smoky chipotle peppers, toasted *comino* (cumin) and crunchy *pepitas* (pumpkin seeds), Parmesan, and tequila reposado will ignite your tastebuds. Try it with grilled meats, fish, or shrimp, add a dollop to soups or frijoles, spread it on pizza or smoked turkey sandwiches, or toss with pasta or potato salad.

At your next party, serve a platter of roasted new potatoes accompanied with a bowl of Si Pica thinned with sour cream for dunking. This pesto also flavors another fiesta favorite, Torta Chipotle, a chilled cheese torta (recipe page 119).

4 cloves garlic
1¼ cups fresh cilantro, tightly packed
½ teaspoon *comino* (cumin)
½ teaspoon dried oregano
¾ cup *pepitas* (pumpkin seeds), toasted
⅓ cup sun-dried tomatoes packed in olive oil, chopped
2 tablespoons red onion, chopped
1 7-ounce can whole chipotle peppers in *adobo* sauce
3 tablespoons reposado or gold tequila
1 cup grated Parmesan cheese
2 tablespoons grated Romano cheese
¾ cup olive oil

In a food processor, grind garlic and cilantro; add cumin, oregano, pepitas, tomatoes, and onion. Add the chipotles (reserving 2 of the chiles for other uses), the tequila, and cheeses. Slowly pour in the olive oil to form a thick paste; do not over process. This is best made a day in advance of serving. Keeps for several weeks in the refrigerator and may be frozen.

Note: Pepitas are available in specialty and health food stores. Unsalted, roasted sunflower seeds may be substituted—both become rancid easily, so make sure that they are fresh; store in the refrigerator.

Makes 2¾ cups

SMOKY CHIPOTLE MARINADE

This smoke-and-fire marinade lights up grilled pork chops, shrimp, or fish. Rub on poultry (and under the skin) before roasting.

3 tablespoons Smoky Chipotle and Toasted Pepita Pesto
2 tablespoons gold tequila
2 tablespoons fresh lime juice
1 tablespoon olive oil
salt and feshly ground pepper to taste

Mix pesto, tequila, and lime juice in a small bowl, and slowly whisk in the olive oil and the salt and pepper. Makes about ½ cup.

Viva Nuevo Mexico
(Roasted Green Chile and Pecan Pesto)

This recipe was inspired by a Christmas gift sent to me by my brother Stuart, a farmer in Mesilla, New Mexico. A five-pound bag of shelled pecans and a bag of his roasted New Mexican green chiles delighted me when I opened the box. He flame-roasts his chiles in the field, then vacuum-packs them to ensure freshness (see Resources).

Spread this pesto on sandwiches, croutons, corn on the cob, or grilled eggplant. Add a spoonful to hearty soups, hot pastas, sautéed vegetables, or mushroom caps before broiling, or use it in a savory vinaigrette or marinade. It is an essential ingredient in Torta Rancho Mesilla, a layered cheese terrine (recipe page 119).

4–6 cloves garlic
2 serranos, chopped (optional)
¾ cup Italian parsley, tightly packed
2 cups fresh cilantro, tightly packed
¼ cup fresh oregano *or* 2 teaspoons dried oregano
½ teaspoon lime zest
2 teaspoons lime juice
3 New Mexico green chiles, roasted, peeled, seeded, and stemmed (page 113)
2 tablespoons tequila (preferably flavored with chile peppers, (page 64)
¾ cup toasted pecans (page 119)
¾ cup freshly grated Parmesan cheese
2 tablespoons grated Romano cheese
¾ cup olive oil

In a food processor, mince garlic, serrano chiles, parsley, cilantro, and oregano. Add lime zest and juice, green chiles, and tequila; mix in pecans and cheeses. With the motor running, slowly add olive oil to form a thick paste. Keeps for several weeks in the refrigerator or freezer.

Note: For a dry pesto to use as a stuffing for pork or beef tenderloin, chicken breasts, or mushrooms, omit olive oil when grinding ingredients together.

Makes about 2 cups

Torta Rancho Mesilla
(Chilled Cheese Torta Layered with Roasted Green Chile and Pecan Pesto)

This recipe is named for my brother Stuart's ranch since he keeps me supplied with chiles and pecans year-round. Strips of roasted New Mexico chile peppers criss-cross the top of this South-western-inspired torta, which may be prepared up to three days before serving, making entertaining easy. As a first course, the torta may be sliced and served on a bed of field greens accompanied by garlicky croutons (page 137) and Fiesta Frijoles (page 132) and garnished with herbs or sunny nasturtium blossoms.

3 fresh New Mexico green chiles, roasted, peeled, seeded, and cut into rajas (see page 113)

1 large red bell pepper, roasted, peeled, seeded, and cut into rajas

½ cup pecans, toasted and chopped; pine nuts may be substituted

¾ pound provolone, thinly sliced

1 recipe Queso Sabroso (page 117)

1 generous cup Roasted Green Chile and Pecan Pesto (page 118)

garnishes and accompaniments: fresh sprigs of oregano, Italian parsley, and/or cilantro; nasturtium blossoms; toasted pecans; homemade garlicky croutons; homemade tostada chips (page 116); Fiesta Frijoles (page 132)

Line a 5-cup loaf pan with plastic wrap, leaving a 1-inch overhang on all sides. Cover the bottom of the pan with 3 overlapping slices of provolone; press more slices lightly onto the sides of the pan to form a shell (trim if necessary). Combine the red and green rajas, reserving the prettiest ones for garnishing the top layer.

In a medium-sized bowl, combine the Queso Sabroso and the chile-pecan pesto with an electric mixer. Evenly spread one-third of it as the first layer, then arrange one-third of the rajas on top of that in a criss-cross pattern and sprinkle with ¼ cup nuts. Cover with another layer of provolone slices, pressing down firmly before spreading half of the remaining goat cheese/pesto filling, half of the rajas, and remaining pecans. Repeat the layering, with a goat cheese/pesto layer on the top. Garnish with the remaining rajas arranged in a criss-cross pattern. Cover tightly with plastic wrap and chill overnight or for as many as 3 days.

To serve, carefully remove the torta from the mold and peel away the plastic wrap. Place on a platter adorned with the garnishes and accompaniments of your choice.

Serves 12 or more

Smoky Chipotle Torta
(Chilled Cheese Torta Layered with Smoky Chipotle and Toasted Pepita Pesto)

Chile and tequila aficionados have one thing in common: passion! This feisty cheese torta may require icy shots of tequila to cool the palate! Serve with tostada chips or croutons, accompanied by bowls of flavorful salsas.

½ cup toasted pepitas or unsalted toasted sunflower seeds

¾ pound provolone, thinly sliced

¾ cup Smoky Chipotle and Toasted Pepita Pesto (see page 118)

1 recipe Queso Sabroso

⅓ cup finely shredded Parmesan cheese

1 red bell pepper, roasted, peeled, and cut into rajas (see page 113)

garnishes: fresh cilantro or oregano sprigs, epazote leaves, sun-dried tomatoes, whole chipotles in adobo, or tostada chips

Line a 5-cup loaf pan with plastic wrap, leaving a 1-inch overhang on all sides. Cover the bottom of the pan with 3 overlapping slices of provolone; press more slices lightly onto the sides to form a shell (trim if necessary).

In a medium-sized bowl, combine Smoky Chipotle Pesto and Queso Sabroso with an electric mixer. Evenly spread ⅓ of it as the first layer in the provolone shell, and sprinkle with ⅓ of the Parmesan and ½ of the toasted pepitas. Cover with another layer of provolone slices, pressing down firmly before spreading ½ of remaining goat cheese filling and Parmesan, and all remaining pepitas. Cover with a final layer of provolone slices, pressing down firmly before spreading the final layer of goat cheese/pesto. Sprinkle with remaining Parmesan, and press red rajas into a decorative design. Cover tightly and chill overnight.

To serve, lift torta from the mold and carefully peel away the plastic wrap. Place on a platter garnished with fresh herbs and croutons or tostada chips. If desired, accompany with Fiesta Frijoles. Serve within 3 days.

Note: Have a deli slice the provolone into ⅛-inch slices, placing waxed paper between them to prevent their sticking together. Mozzarella may be substituted—slice it slightly thicker.

Torta may also be served inverted on a platter. To do so, add another layer of provolone and fold edges over. Chill before inverting onto platter.

Serves 12 or more

TOASTING NUTS/SEEDS

Place pecans, pine nuts, almonds, pumpkin or sunflower seeds on a baking sheet in a 325°F preheated oven and toast until golden brown, turning occasionally. When done, remove from the pan to prevent overcooking.

Queso Flameado
(Melted Cheese Flambéed in Tequila)

Jalisco's famed melted cheese dish, *queso fundido* is better known as *queso flameado* in the northern state of Monterrey. Sometimes it is flambéed at the table with brandy. I use tequila instead, giving a much more authentic flavor to this traditional Mexican dish. Dim the lights for a spectacular presentation. This cheese dish makes a wonderful accompaniment for grilled meats, along with small bowls of colorful salsas and other condiments. Serve with hot tortillas.

12 ounces creamy white cheese such as queso Chihuahua, queso blanco, queso asadero, Monterey Jack, Muenster, or mozzarella (or a combination of any), grated

1 tablespoon canola or safflower oil

1 tablespoon butter

½ large white onion, cut into thin slices

2 cloves garlic

4 New Mexico green chile peppers or poblanos, roasted, peeled, seeded, and cut into *rajas* (see page 113)

2 tablespoons gold or reposado tequila plus 2 tablespoons tequila to flambé

salt and pepper to taste

condiments: chopped tomatoes, avocado wedges drizzled with fresh lime juice, chopped green onions, chopped fresh cilantro, or your favorite salsa

12 flour or corn tortillas

Briefly sauté the onion and garlic in the oil and butter; add the chile peppers, 2 tablespoons tequila, salt and pepper to taste, stirring until the tequila is absorbed. Do not overcook.

Place the grated cheese in a shallow 9 x 12-inch earthenware dish or in 6 individual flame-proof ramekins. Top with the pepper/onion mixture. Place 6 inches under a preheated broiler and heat until bubbly, melted and lightly browned (about 4–5 minutes).

Dim the lights and remove cheese from oven. Briefly heat the remaining 2 tablespoons tequila in a small, heavy saucepan. To serve at the table, carefully ignite warmed tequila as you pour it from the saucepan over the sizzling cheese. Accompany with small bowls of condiments and a basket of hot flour or corn tortillas.

Variations: Sauté a handful of sliced mushrooms with the pepper/onion mixture. Crumbled fried *chorizo* (spicy Mexican pork sausage) may be used instead of the pepper/onion mixture; use slightly less than ½ pound chorizo.

Serves 6

Baja Bravo

(Marinated Cheese with Tequila, Anchovies, and Jalapeño-Stuffed Green Olives)

Many years ago, a friend and I drove a pickup truck across a deserted mountain road in Baja, California del Norte, to the Pacific Ocean. We had packed some ripe tomatoes, a slab of creamy cheese, canned sardines, and some crusty *bolillos* (Mexican rolls) for what we thought would be an afternoon picnic. It took many more hours than we expected to reach the sea, driving up and down a treacherous winding dirt road. When we finally had our picnic, it was on a desolate strand, with warming shots of tequila and the full moon as our only company. Not daring the drive back, we spent the night in the back of the truck.

This recipe recreates for me a magical evening, and I offer it for kindred souls with a passion for bold flavors and adventures. Serve Baja Bravo with shots of ice-cold tequila or margaritas and slather on croutons garnished with fresh basil or rosemary or stuff it into hollowed bolillos or baguettes.

For the marinade:

3 cloves garlic, minced

1 tablespoon concentrated Italian tomato paste

3 tablespoons tequila reposado (part chile pepper-flavored if desired)

3 tablespoons capers, drained

1 tablespoon balsamic vinegar

¼–½ teaspoon crushed dried red chile pepper (optional)

2 teaspoons fresh rosemary, minced

4–6 flat fillets of anchovies, chopped

6 tablespoons olive oil

For the tomato-olive mixture:

2 cups ripe Roma tomatoes, chopped, lightly salted, and drained in a colander

4 green onions, chopped

15 large green jalapeño-stuffed olives, each cut in half

½ cup fresh basil, chopped

¼ cup fresh cilantro, chopped

3–4 New Mexico green chiles, cut into rajas (see page 113)

8 ounces queso blanco or Monterey Jack, grated

salt and freshly ground pepper to taste, optional

garnishes: shredded Parmesan, whole anchovy fillets, fresh basil or cilantro sprigs, minced rosemary

Prepare the marinade by combining the ingredients in a small bowl, whisking in the olive oil last; set aside.

In a medium-sized bowl, combine tomatoes, green onions, olives, fresh herbs, rajas, jalapeños if using, and cheese, then toss with marinade. Add salt and pepper to taste. Cover (or refrigerate overnight) and allow to sit at room temperature for an hour before serving. Serve with croutons or bread.

Note: Baja Bravo makes a delicious uncooked sauce for pasta in the summertime. The hot pasta will melt the cheese and bring out tequila's flavor. Try it as well on grilled fish or chicken. Serve with shots of ice cold tequila or margaritas. Mound Baja Bravo into a roasted whole poblano for a special presentation (page 126).

Makes 4½ cups

"Pescado"
hand painted wooden fish
Guerrero, Mexico

Salsas y Sorpresas

In Mexico, flavorful table *salsas* make the simplest foods come to life. In a country where tortillas, frijoles, and eggs are a mainstay, salsas offer variety to otherwise mundane meals. Drizzled over tacos, tostadas, frijoles, or meats, salsas enliven traditional fare, adding color, flavor, and texture. I have taken traditional Mexican ingredients and techniques (further enlivening them with a splash of tequila) to create salsas with a contemporary flair.

What I call *sorpresas* or surprises, are confetti-colored concoctions of freshly chopped vegetables and fruits in zesty tequila marinades. They are chunkier and heartier than the table salsas. Spirited, and spicy, they are brimming with color and texture, adding an element of surprise to the fiesta table. They are wonderfully versatile and lend themselves to festive presentations as condiments, relishes, salads, or first courses.

You can serve the *salsas y sorpresas* in bowls surrounding a platter of grilled meats, chicken, or fish. Let your guests layer crispy tostadas or fill folded warm tortillas with a variety of these tasty morsels, using imagination in their creations.

Salsas

These sassy salsas will make even everyday meals come to life!

Salsa Jardinera
(Garden Green Cilantro Salsa with Tequila)

This bright green aromatic salsa, brimming with herbs fresh from the garden is always at hand in my refrigerator.

Drizzle it over chilled asparagus, roasted new potatoes, and sliced garden tomatoes. Use it as a marinade for grilled shrimp or meats or roasted chicken (and as a marinade before grilling). For a quick meal, heat a quesadilla made with mild goat cheese on the griddle; stuff with an assortment of field greens and grated raw vegetables liberally doused with *Salsa Jardinera*.

6 cloves garlic
3 serrano chiles, roughly chopped
1½ cups fresh cilantro, tightly packed
¼ cup fresh mint, tightly packed
2 teaspoons dried oregano
1 cup Italian parsley, tightly packed
2 fresh bay leaves
2 teaspoons fresh rosemary, removed from stem
4 large tomatillos, husks removed, rinsed, and quartered
2 teaspoons whole coriander seeds
2 dried red chiles de árbol
1 teaspoon whole white peppercorns
1 cup rice wine vinegar
grated zest and juice of 1 large orange
6 tablespoons reposado tequila
1 teaspoon salt
1 scant cup olive oil

Rinse the fresh herbs and pat dry. In the bowl of a food processor, mince garlic and serranos. Add herbs and tomatillos. Grind the spices in a spice grinder and add to herb mixture with vinegar, orange zest and juice, tequila, and salt. Slowly add the olive oil. Refrigerate overnight before adjusting flavors—it will thicken slightly.

Note: Fresh cilantro, mint, and parsley are essential to this recipe. However, in a pinch, the other herbs may be used dried. A good rule of thumb is to use three times as much of the fresh herb as dried. Try using a tequila infused with fresh herbs or citrus in this recipe.

Makes 3½ cups

Chimichurri Rojo
(Salsa de Chile de Árbol)

After showing me his distillery, Antonio Nuñez, owner of Tequila El Viejito, took me to the Restaurant Campestre on the outskirts of Atotonilco. The gaily painted patio and open air bar overlooks hillsides glistening with rows of silver agave. We sipped a *cazuela* (page 94), a refreshing tequila drink served in a glazed earthenware bowl, while the aroma of sizzling garlic made us ravenous.

At the restaurant, owners Lulu and Luis Navarro combine traditional ingredients and techniques with original ideas and contemporary presentations. They lovingly prepare their dishes, garnishing them in the same vivid colors of the hand-woven tablecloths. Fresh pink unpeeled shrimp or beef tenderloin tips *a la parilla* (seared on a hot griddle)arrived on platters adorned with sliced beets and carrots, grilled plantains, red onion rings, and shredded cabbage. Bowls of *frijoles refritos*, freshly made tostada chips, *queso fresco*, *arroz*, and plenty of hot tortillas followed, along with shots of tequila and sangrita.

Luis brought a bowl of his *chimichurri* , a salsa fashioned after a garlicky green herb and vinegar table sauce that accompanies grilled meats in Argentina. His version is red and flavored with fiery chiles de árbol instead of the traditional green herbs. To everyone's surprise, I added a little bit of tequila to the chimichurri and it was delicious! We dunked shrimp in it, drizzled it on the beans and the beef, and spread it on the croutons that Lulu brought to the table in a small basket.

This recipe keeps indefinitely in the refrigerator, on hand to perk up any tortilla-based recipe, roasted chicken, grilled meats, eggs, or even chunky mashed potatoes with chopped parsley. You can also add it to marinades, sauces, and salad dressings. But remember, a little goes a long way. It's hot!

25 dried chiles de árbol (approximately 1 ounce)

5 cloves garlic

2 tablespoons Italian parsley

2 tablespoons fresh cilantro

⅓ cup cane vinegar or rice wine vinegar

¼ cup gold tequila

½ teaspoon dried oregano

1 teaspoon salt

½ cup olive oil

On a hot griddle, briefly toast the chiles. Discard the stems and some of the seeds and grind the chiles in a blender with the garlic, parsley, and cilantro. Add the vinegar, tequila, oregano, and salt and slowly drizzle in the olive oil.

Makes 1¾ cups

TO ROAST TOMATILLOS

Place the tomatillos in their husks on a preheated comal or griddle. Roast them, turning often, until the husks begin to brown and the tomatillo has become soft (about 8 minutes). Remove the husks before using in sauces.

Salsa Borracha
(Drunken Sauce with Chiles-Colorado)

In Mexico, Salsa Borracha is traditionally made with the dark and mild chile pasilla and flavored with pulque. My version features the earthy and robust flavor of dried red New Mexico chiles ground with tart roasted tomatillos and garlic and spiked with tequila. Use it as a table sauce or as a dip for tostada chips. Rub it on chicken (and under the skin) before roasting for color and flavor (see Pollo Enchilado, page 140), or offer it as a condiment for hamburgers, grilled meats, shrimp, or black beans.

5 tablespoons reposado tequila

8–10 plump tomatillos

10–12 New Mexico dried red chiles colorados or guajillos

4 cloves garlic

¼–½ cup water (approximately)

½ white onion, chopped

½ teaspoon salt

3–4 tablespoons cilantro, chopped

In a small heavy saucepan, briefly heat the tequila to a boil to burn off some of the alcohol; remove from the heat. Roast tomatillos on a hot griddle; set aside and then toast chiles on the griddle for about 15 seconds a side. Do not burn or they will taste bitter. Remove and discard the chiles' seeds, stems, and fibrous veins. Tear chiles into small pieces and place in a food processor or blender with garlic and tomatillos. Add just enough water to make a thick paste, then add tequila and salt. Allow the sauce to mellow for several hours, or preferably overnight. Before serving, sprinkle with onion and cilantro. This sauce keeps well for several weeks in the refrigerator.

Makes 2 cups

Salsa Rosita
(Pink Pomegranate Salad Dressing)

Fresh pomegranate seeds (fresh raspberries may be used in a pinch) give a tart and tangy flavor and rosy pink color to this celebratory salad dressing, while flecks of cayenne, lime zest, and a splash of tequila give it a Mexican flair. The slightly nutty yet delicate flavor of avocado oil makes this dressing especially elegant for any fruit salad. For a fiesta salad, serve segments of ruby red grapefruit and navel oranges and avocado wedges sprinkled with fresh pomegranate seeds, pink peppercorns, or raspberries on a bed of red-tipped lettuce. Serve this in the fall when citrus and pomegranates are in season, or during summer's raspberry season.

3 tablespoons fresh pomegranate seeds or 15 ripe raspberries
3 tablespoons raspberry vinegar
1 tablespoon freshly squeezed lime juice
3 tablespoons 100 percent agave silver tequila or tequila infused with orange peel
5 tablespoon chopped red onion
¼ teaspoon crushed cayenne
Coarsely grated zest of 1 lime
1 tablespoon granulated sugar
¼ teaspoon salt
¼ teaspoon freshly ground pink peppercorns
½ cup plus 1 tablespoon avocado, safflower, or sunflower oil

Combine pomegranate seeds (or berries), vinegar, lime juice, and tequila in a blender or food processor and purée briefly until bright pink. Strain through a fine mesh strainer, using the back of a spoon to press out all of the juice.

Rinse out processor bowl and dry, then add onion, crushed red pepper, lime zest, sugar, salt, and peppercorns along with "pink"-tequila mixture and process until well blended. With the motor running, add remaining oil in a steady stream. Adjust flavorings, adding more lime or sugar as needed. Pour into a jar and refrigerate—it will thicken. The salad dressing keeps for a week.

Note: Avocado oil is very low in saturated fat, making it a healthy oil alternative. If desired, add tangerine segments, and/or chopped jicama to the salad.

Makes 1 generous cup

EQUIVALENTS

1 medium lime = 1 teaspoon zest, 2 tablespoons juice

1 Mexican limón = ½ tablespoon

1 medium navel orange = 2 teaspoons zest, ⅜ cup juice

1 small jicama = 1 pound, 5 cups

1 small mango = ½ pound, ½ cup

1 medium red bell pepper = 1 cup, medium dice

1 purple onion = ½ cup, chopped

1 ear fresh corn = 1 cup kernels

Madrugada
(Sunset Habanero-Carrot Salsa)

The Penn brothers seem to grow every chile pepper imaginable on their farm in the Texas Hill Country, supplying restaurants across the United States with their bounty. This bright orange carrot salsa looks innocuous but "should be used at great personal risk," as Tom Penn jokes when describing his creation. It comes in handy the morning after a night of tequila debauchery: your burning tongue will make you forget about your throbbing head. Habanero enthusiasts will eat this slightly sweet yet ferocious salsa on everything—grilled swordfish or red snapper, sautéed shrimp, or roasted pork. Spread it on pizza or sandwiches, or add it to sauces and marinades.

3–5 habanero or Scotch Bonnet chile peppers, stemmed and seeded
4 cups carrots, scraped and shredded
⅔ cup grated onion
5 large cloves garlic, minced
juice of 2 limes
2 tablespoons vinegar
2 tablespoons tequila reposado
1 teaspoon salt
1½ tablespoons chopped fresh cilantro

Roast whole peppers on a grill or in an oven until evenly charred. Coarsely purée in blender with remaining ingredients, adding cilantro at the end. Keeps for several weeks in the refrigerator.

Makes 3–4 pints

LUCINDA'S COCINA TIPS

★ Rub hands lightly with oil and lime juice before working with fresh hot chiles to prevent stinging. Rub fresh lime juice on hands to remove garlic odor.

★ Do not serve or prepare dishes with acidic ingredients in Mexican *cazuelas* (earthenware dishes) as they may contain lead.

"margaritas"
margarita is
the Spanish name
for daisy

FESTIVE PRESENTATIONS

Sorpresas can be sprinkled on tostadas, beans, or grilled meats. For a special effect, mound the sorpresas into any of the following to serve as a condiment, salad, or as a first course:

Corn Husk Boats (for 6)

Soak 8 dried corn husks (used to make tamales) in water for several hours; pat dry. Tear 2 of the husks into ½-inch strips for tying the ends of the corn husk boats. Place a whole small lime in the center of each moistened husk and wrap the husk around the lime, tying at both ends with the torn strips. Allow to dry, then remove the lime, leaving a cavity for the filling.

Poblano Peppers

Roast and peel poblano peppers (see page 113), leaving the stems intact. Carefully make about a 2 ½-inch slit down the center of each poblano and remove seeds; mound the filling within. Chill before serving. For added flavor, marinate the poblanos in olive oil, vinegar, minced garlic, salt, and pepper for an hour before stuffing. You may wish to decrease the chile peppers called for in the recipe (New Mexico peppers may be used but tear easily when stuffing).

Baby Pumpkins

Cut off the tops of miniature pumpkins and carefully hollow them out, then fill.

Tortilla Cups

With a 3-inch scalloped cookie cutter, cut circles out of 6 corn tortillas. In a deep-fat fryer or heavy saucepan, heat enough vegetable oil to 375°F for deep frying. Hold the tortilla down in hot oil with a small ladle, and fry it until it's golden brown and its edges curl up to form a cup shape around the ladle. (Specially designed devices are also available for this purpose.) Remove from the hot oil and invert to drain on paper towels. These "cups" may be stored in an airtight container at room temperature for up to 3 days. Heat in a low oven for a few minutes to recrisp. Fill just prior to serving.

PREPARING THE VEGETABLES

Black Beans

For cooking instructions see page 130. The black beans should be slightly firm in texture and not overcooked; for a smoky variation, cook beans with 2–3 whole dried chipotle peppers. If canned black beans are used (two 16-ounce cans), rinse them and drain well before using.

Tomatoes

Sprinkle chopped tomatoes lightly with salt, and drain in a colander to release excess moisture before adding to the recipe. If recipe is held overnight, add tomatoes a few hours prior to serving.

Corn

To cold-toss corn kernels, blanch for 30 seconds in rapidly boiling water. Immediately refresh in a colander set in a bowl of ice water. If frozen corn is used, simply thaw and drain well before using.

Sorpresas

These "no-cook" sorpresas are ideal for warm weather menus: lively, refreshing, and low in fat, they make healthy and filling one-bowl meals. I often accompany them with a quesadilla, a tortilla folded over a slice of creamy white cheese and briefly heated on a hot griddle. They are also delicious served as salad on a bed of greens.

The following recipes were designed in party portions but may be easily halved. When preparing *sorpresas*, mound the colorful ingredients in the mixing bowl as you chop them; gently toss to avoid bruising the tender fruits and vegetables; do not stir too much. To bring out the flavors, chill them for several hours or overnight, gently tossing occasionally. Serve with a slotted spoon to drain excess marinade.

Pico De Gallo
(Bite of the Rooster)

Throughout Mexico, street vendors sell slices of jícama and juicy pineapple and orange halves sprinkled with fresh lime juice and dusted with chile powder, a cool and refreshing alternative to American fast food. This same combination is also served on a platter, cut into bite-sized chunks and accompanied by shots of tequila. As you pick up a piece with your thumb and forefinger, your remaining fingers resemble a rooster's comb, and as you plop the chile-dusted morsel into your mouth, you get the "bite of the rooster," or *pico de gallo*. Great with icy shots of tequila.

I have embellished this traditional favorite with a spicy tequila marinade. Serve as a salad on a bed of greens, as a lively accompaniment for grilled fish or chicken, or by the bowlful—especially for breakfast. What a way to start the day!

For the marinade:

4 tablespoons silver tequila, or tequila infused with orange peel or pineapple (see page 61)

3 tablespoons fresh orange juice

3 tablespoons fresh lime juice

½ teaspoon crushed dried red chile

½ teaspoon salt

For the chopped ingredients:

1 medium jícama (about 2 pounds), peeled and cut into bite-sized chunks

1 fresh pineapple, peeled and cut into bite-sized chunks

4 navel oranges, peeled and cut into bite-sized chunks

2 serranos, chopped

1 small red onion, chopped

garnishes: pure chile powder, pomegranate seeds, or nasturtium blossoms

Prepare the marinade by whisking together the ingredients in a small bowl; set aside. In a large glass bowl, toss the chopped ingredients gently, then add the marinade, toss again, and chill for several hours, stirring occasionally. Drain excess liquid (and drink!) Add more lime juice if needed and dust with pure chile powder before serving. Sprinkle with pomegranate seeds or nasturtium blossoms when in season.

Makes about 8 cups

gaily painted
clay chickens
Jalisco,
Mexico

Barca De Oro
(Golden Mango Salsa in Citrusy Tequila Marinade)

Mango trees abound in many parts of Mexico, where sometimes a bite into a slice of a green mango accompanies a shot of tequila in place of a wedge of lime. On those lucky days when I catch a *dorado* (mahi-mahi) while fishing in the Sea of Cortéz in Baja, I compliment its delicate flavor with this refreshing medley of ingredients mounded in a corn husk *barca* or boat (see page 126).

Try it with grilled chicken or fish, pork tenderloin or lamb chops. Eat it by the bowlful, use it as a garnish for black beans, or serve it as a salad on a bed of greens, garnished with fresh mint.

For the marinade:

3 tablespoons tequila infused with orange peel or premium silver tequila
3 tablespoons fresh orange juice
3 tablespoons fresh lime juice
¼ teaspoon salt
¼ teaspoon crushed dried chile de árbol or cayenne

For the mango mixture:

3 medium mangoes, peeled and chopped into medium dice (about 2 cups)
1½ cups jicama, peeled and chopped into medium dice
2 fresh hot peppers, preferably red-ripened jalapeños or fresnos (serranos or 1 habanero may also be used), minced
¼ cup red onion, chopped
pure mild chile powder

In a small bowl, mix together ingredients for marinade; set aside.

Combine chopped mangoes, jícama, chile peppers, and onion; toss gently in marinade. Chill for several hours then dust with chile powder before serving.

Makes 4 cups

¡Ay Caramba! Coleslaw
(Thai/Tex Tequila Coleslaw)

Texas and Thailand have two things in common: hot summers and people with a passion for spicy flavorings, such as garlic, ginger, hot chiles, and cilantro.

Combining these spices with tequila and a fiesta of colorful vegetables is sure to get a lot of attention at the table. As a condiment for wild game, roasted meats, or barbecued chicken—or by the bowlful sprinkled with honey-roasted peanuts this truly "pickled" coleslaw/relish is a winner.

For the marinade:

3 tablespoons gold tequila
2 teaspoons grated orange zest
3 tablespoons fresh orange juice
2 tablespoons fresh lime juice
2 tablespoons rice wine vinegar
½ teaspoon curry powder
1 teaspoon whole coriander seeds, freshly ground
½ teaspoon whole peppercorn mélange, freshly ground
2 teaspoons dried mustard
1 tablespoon brown sugar
¼ teaspoon crushed chile de árbol or cayenne (optional)
1-inch piece of ginger, peeled
2 cloves garlic, peeled
1 serrano, stemmed and cut in half
1 tablespoon fresh cilantro, finely chopped
1 tablespoon fresh mint, finely chopped
½ teaspoon salt
⅓ cup cold-pressed peanut oil

For the slaw:

½ large purple cabbage (about 1¼ pounds), cut in thin slices
1 red bell pepper, julienned
1 yellow bell pepper, julienned
2 carrots, grated
2 ribs of celery, chopped
1 cup red onion, chopped
½ cup fresh cilantro, chopped
3 tablespoons chopped fresh mint
1 fresh serrano, chopped
garnishes: honey-roasted peanuts, lime wedges, fresh cilantro or mint sprigs

In a small bowl, combine tequila, orange zest and juice, lime juice, and rice vinegar with the curry powder, mustard, ground spices, brown sugar, and crushed chile.

In a food processor, mince the ginger, garlic, serrano, cilantro, and mint. Add the tequila mixture and the salt, then, with the machine still running, slowly add the oil in a steady stream. Set aside.

Mix together the slaw ingredients in a large bowl; toss gently with the marinade. Chill for several hours, tossing occasionally. Before serving, garnish with fresh sprigs of cilantro or mint, surround with lime wedges, and sprinkle liberally with honey-roasted peanuts. The slaw is pretty mounded in hollowed-out orange halves when serving as a condiment. Serve within a day or two.

Makes about 6 cups

Nuevo Mundo
(New World Salsa)

In early summer, there's nothing better than sweet corn right off the cob. Combining it with tomatoes, squash, chile peppers, and tequila pays due homage to all of these gifts from the New World. Mexicans often pair sweet corn with *chayote*, a pale green pear-shaped vegetable that tastes like a squash. Chayote is often available in North American markets and lends its crunchy texture to this colorful medley (zucchini will do in a pinch). A tequila marinade, redolent of fresh herbs and spices makes this a great condiment for roasted turkey, grilled fish, wild game, or black beans. It is delicious by the bowlful, layered on tostadas, or stuffed in avocado or tomato halves as a salad.

For the marinade:

5 tablespoons 100 percent agave reposado tequila

2 tablespoons minced shallots

3 tablespoons white wine vinegar

½ teaspoon freshly ground coriander seeds

1 teaspoon dried oregano

1 teaspoon brown sugar

5 tablespoons mild-flavored oil such as safflower, sunflower, or avocado

½ teaspoon salt

freshly ground pepper to taste

For the vegetables:

4 medium ears of fresh sweet white corn, cut off the cob (about 3 cups), cold-tossed (see page 126) and drained

2 medium chayote or zucchini squash, cut into medium dice, (about 3 cups), cold-tossed (see page 126) and drained

1 small red onion, chopped

1 red bell pepper, chopped

2–4 jalapeños

½ cup or more any combination of fresh marjoram, cilantro, oregano

1 tablespoon marigold mint, optional

1½ cups teardrop or cherry tomatoes, halved

½ pound pepper Jack cheese, cut into ⅜-inch cubes (optional)

3 green onions, chopped

garnishes: vine-ripened golden pear or cherry tomatoes, red onion rings, marigold mint sprigs, nasturtium flowers, or avocado wedges drizzled with fresh lime juice

In a small, heavy saucepan, mix the tequila with the shallots, vinegar, and coriander seeds; bring to a boil and briefly heat to evaporate some of the alcohol, leaving the natural sweetness of the agave. Allow to cool, then add the oregano, brown sugar, salt, and pepper; whisk in the oil.

In a large bowl, combine the chopped vegetables and herbs and toss gently with the marinade. Allow to chill for several hours, tossing occasionally. Before serving, toss in the pepper Jack cheese and the green onions.

Note: Mexican marigold mint, known as *yerbanís* in Mexico, is at once reminiscent of anise, tarragon, and mint. Mexicans usually use it medicinally, but they sometimes use it to flavor fresh corn and squash. It gives this dish its special character, especially in the fall when its golden marigold-like flowers may also be used as garnish.

If using this dish as an accompaniment for the cheese *tortas*, omit the pepper Jack, adding ½ cup rajas to recipe (page 133).

Use young and tender thin-skinned chayote, do not peel. To cold-toss chayote or zucchini, blanch in rapidly boiling water for about 1½ minutes; immediately refresh in an ice-water bath.

Makes 10 cups (with the cheese)

Manzanita
(Green Apple-Mexican Marigold Mint Salsa)

Whenever I need food that will sing to my soul, I head to Castle Hill Restaurant in Austin, Texas. Chef David Dailey's imaginative combinations of ingredients always hit the spot. David serves this crunchy green apple salsa as a relish topping grilled salmon on a bed of greens dressed in a balsamic vinaigrette. Warm and regal colors and vibrant flavors make this a delightful autumn relish—try it with sharp Cheddar cheese and crackers. It is a must for *Puerco con Miel y Mostaza* (page 140), wild game, or the Thanksgiving turkey.

3 tablespoons golden raisins

3 tablespoons gold tequila

¼ cup sun-dried tomatoes, packed in olive oil, diced (do not drain oil)

1¼ cup jicama, cut into medium dice

¾ cup red onion, cut into medium dice

2 Granny Smith apples, unpeeled, cut into medium dice

1 tablespoon fresh mint or Mexican marigold mint, chopped

juice of 2 limes

2 fresh red-ripened jalapeños or fresno chiles, minced

¼ teaspoon powdered cinnamon

2–3 teaspoons ground ancho or pure mild New Mexico chile powder

salt to taste

handful of toasted walnuts or pecans, coarsely chopped (optional)

Plump the raisins in the tequila while chopping the remaining ingredients. Combine all ingredients in a medium-sized bowl, reserving the toasted nuts to sprinkle on top just prior to serving. May be made the day before serving.

Note: Mexican marigold mint adds a unique flavor to this salsa.

Makes about 4½ cups

FIESTA FRIJOLES

A pot of *frijoles* (beans) livens up the buffet table, providing fun and filling party fare. Let guests select from a variety of garnishes served in small bowls: grated cheese, chopped tomatoes, green onions, serranos, avocado chunks, chipotles in adobo, or a colorful sorpresa (see page 127). I collect tiny wooden and ceramic bowls for salt, dried oregano, and crushed dried red chile for sprinkling into individual bowls and provide a bottle of chile-pepper flavored tequila on hand for those who want an extra splash of flavor.

For me, a hearty bowl of frijoles with a chunk of cornbread or a quesadilla is a meal in itself. Tequila's innate peppery nature adds character to beans and legumes, and cooking them in a clay pot imparts earthiness, authenticity, and depth of flavor.

Cooking Beans

I do not soak frijoles before cooking. Should you need to add more liquid while cooking them, always add hot water to keep the beans from bursting; too much liquid will dilute their flavor. Only add salt during the last 30 minutes of cooking to prevent their toughening. Epazote, the "bean herb," is a flavorful and helpful addition to the frijoles toward the end of cooking, and it may improve your social life (see page 132).

To vary the taste of the frijoles, you can add two or more whole dried chiles such as *chiles colorados* or smoky chipotles to the pot while cooking. *Chile pasado* (roasted, peeled, and sun-dried New Mexico chile) gives a concentrated chile flavor that is both hot and slightly sweet (see Resources). Cooking the frijoles the day before serving them results in a thicker broth and allows the beans to absorb more flavor.

FRIJOLES NEGROS

For a tasty bean dip or layer for tostadas, drain beans, reserving the broth. Purée to desired consistency in a food procesor or blender with enough of the reserved broth, 1 bunch chopped greeen onions, 2–4 jalapenos, serranos or chipotles in adobo, and ½ cup shredded Parmesan. Serve in a dish garnished with bands of Salsa Borracha (page 123) and shredded Parmesan.

Frijoles Borrachos a La Charra
(Drunken Beans Cowgirl-Style)

These ranch-style beans can be a meal in themselves. Flavored with bacon and beer and a hearty tomato salsa splashed with tequila, they are a tasty accompaniment to barbecue and delicious as well for breakfast. Serve with hot flour or corn tortillas or cornbread.

For the frijoles:

1 pound pinto beans, picked over and rinsed
1 teaspoon whole cumin
1 teaspoon crumbled dried oregano
2 cloves garlic
2 dried chiles, optional
1 Mexican beer (12 ounces), such as Bohemia or Dos XX, room temperature
½ pound bacon, cut into ½-inch pieces
3 sprigs fresh epazote or 1 tablespoon dried, optional
1 teaspoon salt

For the salsa:

2 tablespoons bacon fat or oil
3 cloves garlic, chopped
1 white onion, chopped
4 ripe medium tomatoes, chopped
2–4 serrano chiles, chopped
1 teaspoon crumbled dried oregano
salt to taste
½ cup reposado or gold tequila
condiments: bowls of freshly chopped cilantro, epazote, onion, and/or serrano chiles and small bowls of dried oregano and salt

Place beans in an earthenware *olla* (clay bean pot) or other large pot. Add cumin, oregano, garlic, and (optional) chile peppers; add beer and enough water to cover beans by about 2 inches. Bring to a boil; reduce heat and simmer, covered, for about 1 hour, or until beans are almost tender.

Meanwhile, fry bacon until crisp. Drain, reserving 2 tablespoons bacon fat. Add bacon to beans along with epazote and 1 teaspoon salt. Simmer, uncovered, for about another half hour.

Prepare the salsa by sautéing the garlic and onion in the reserved bacon fat; add the tomatoes, serranos, oregano, and salt to taste and simmer for 6-8 minutes. Set aside.

Add the tomato salsa and the tequila to the beans and simmer for 15 minutes just prior to serving. Serve with bowls of condiments at the table.

Serves 8–10

Variation: Try adding 2–3 dried chipotle peppers while cooking the beans to give them a smoky flavor, especially if the bacon is omitted; use olive oil instead of bacon fat.

Beans may be cooked the night before; add the tomato salsa and heat before serving.

Buena Suerte
(Good Luck Black-eyed Peas in Sweet and Spicy Salsa)

Black-eyed peas promise good luck. Whether on New Year's Day or in the summer during the height of their season, these fresh black-eyed peas cooked with smoky bacon and smothered in my grandmother's tomato salsa will certainly bring good cheer. Serve with shots of tequila.

For the black-eyed peas:

2 pounds fresh black-eyed peas
½ pound smoky peppered bacon or 2 meaty ham bones
1 onion, quartered and each quarter studded with 1 clove
2 bay leaves
small handful freshly snipped oregano or savory
3 tablespoons tequila
1 teaspoon salt

For Grandma's sweet and spicy salsa:

3 tablespoons olive oil
1 white onion, chopped
3 cloves garlic, minced
1 red bell pepper, chopped
6 ripe tomatoes, chopped and seeded
2 cloves
¼ teaspoon whole allspice
¼ teaspoon whole peppercorns
1 dried cayenne or chile de árbol
½ teaspoon ground cinnamon
⅓ cup tequila reposado
3 tablespoons red wine vinegar
2 (or more, to taste) teaspoons brown sugar
6 New Mexico or Anaheim green chiles, roasted, peeled, seeded, and cut into rajas (see page 113)
salt to taste
condiments: bowls of chopped onions, chopped serranos or jalapeños, and cilantro, and a bottle of chile pepper – flavored tequila

Place black-eyed peas, bacon, onion, bay leaves, oregano, tequila, and salt in a Dutch oven and cover with water. Bring to a boil, then reduce heat and simmer for 30 minutes; do not overcook. Let cool in broth, then drain away liquid. Cut the meat into bits, discarding fat, and return to the peas.

To make salsa, heat the olive oil in a large pan. Sauté onion until translucent; add garlic and bell pepper and sauté briefly. Add tomatoes and simmer, reducing liquid slightly. Grind cloves, allspice, peppercorns, and chile de arbol in a spice grinder and add them to the pan, along with cinnamon, tequila, vinegar, and brown sugar. Simmer for about 30 minutes, then add green chile rajas and continue to simmer until sauce has thickened. Add more brown sugar if needed and salt to taste.

Just before serving, pour salsa over black-eyed peas and simmer for 10 minutes. Serve warm accompanied by bowls of condiments.

Serves 8–10

Note: Try Grandma's sweet and spicy salsa over hamburgers, eggplant, black beans, okra, zucchini, grilled fish, or pork chops.

Fiesta Frijoles
(Black Beans and Corn in Peppered Tequila Marinade)

This is always a fiesta favorite. The sweet and crunchy flavor of fresh corn kernels combined with earthy black beans, and doused in a spicy tequila marinade is delicious as an appetizer with tostada chips or as a side dish. Loaded with color and flavor, Fiesta Frijoles are perfect for a large gathering and can be made a day in advance. Serve accompanied by redonditas (recipe page 117) or cheese tortas (see page 119), or spooned over pasta.

HOJA SANTA (PIPER AURITUM)

The musky anise flavor of this large heart-shaped leaf complements the earthiness of black beans. I tear a few pieces from one of the large (8- to 10-inch) leaves and add them to the beans the last 30 minutes of cooking. Although difficult to find, *hoja santa* thrives in Southwestern gardens.

For the marinade:

4 cloves garlic, minced

1½ teaspoons cumin seeds, toasted and coarsely ground

2 teaspoons dried oregano

3 tablespoons chile pepper-flavored tequila

4 tablespoons red wine vinegar

2 bay leaves, preferably fresh, crushed

½ teaspoon salt

5 tablespoons olive oil

For the bean mixture:

3½ cups cooked black beans, chilled and drained (see page 126)

4 or more serranos or jalapeños, chopped (or more, to taste)

6 green onions with some of the green tops, chopped

1 cup chopped red onion

½ cup chopped fresh cilantro

2 tablespoons chopped fresh epazote, (optional)

2 cups fresh sweet corn kernels, cold-tossed (see page 126)

6 Roma tomatoes, chopped, lightly salted, and drained in a colander

salt to taste

juice of 1–2 fresh limes

In a small bowl, combine all marinade ingredients except olive oil, then slowly whisk in the oil.

In a large bowl, combine bean-mixture ingredients, then toss with marinade. Chill for several hours or overnight, turning occasionally. (If the recipe is to be held overnight, add corn and tomatoes a few hours before serving.) Drizzle with fresh lime juice and add salt to taste before serving.

Makes 8 cups

Note: You can reserve the corn to use as a golden ring to garnish the black bean mixture instead of incorporating it into the dish. When chile-pepper flavored tequila is not available, simply add ¼-½ teaspoon of crushed dried red pepper to the tequila called for in the recipe.

EPAZOTE (*CHENOPODIUM ABROSIOIDES*): THE "BEAN HERB"

This pungent Mexican herb with deeply serrated leaves and a pungent camphor/minty flavor reputedly prevents the embarrassing consequences of eating beans. It may be used either dried (with stems) or fresh and grows eagerly in North American gardens. It is often cooked with frijoles in Mexico and is sometimes used freshly chopped to garnish them as one would use cilantro.

CALDOS DE COLORES: Colorful Soups

You can serve a filling one-course dinner around a cold or warm soup, creating a fiesta atmosphere by allowing guests to choose from an array of condiments enticingly displayed in bowls, carved gourds, or even shells.

On the table, place small bowls of salt, dried oregano, crushed red chile pepper, and a bottle of chile pepper-flavored tequila for extra seasoning. Baskets of steaming corn tortillas wrapped in bright napkins, cornbread muffins, or bolillos—Mexico's crusty rolls—are perfect accompaniments.

Gazpacho

Gazpacho, the traditional chilled Spanish soup made with tomatoes, peppers, cucumbers, olive oil, and vinegar, is the life of the fiesta when spiked with tequila. Here are three refreshing versions, colorful concoctions made with fresh, hand-diced fruits and vegetables. Serve these summery gazpachos from icy mugs at a stand-up buffet, with an assortment of condiments. Or serve as a first course followed by grilled fish or chicken. Presented in long-stemmed jumbo margarita glasses, gazpacho also makes a lovely luncheon soup.

Gazpacho del Sol
(Golden Gazpacho Spiked with Tequila)

The flavors of this summer soup linger like the memory of a tropical vacation. In Mexico, street vendors sell orange halves and slices of pineapple or jícama, and artistically carved whole mangos—all drizzled with fresh lime juice and dusted with bright red chile powder, an inspiration for this recipe. For a special first-course presentation, dip the rims of chilled goblets into mild chile powder, fill with golden gazpacho, and garnish with a slice of star fruit, the tips dipped in chile powder. Or serve this as a chilled compote, sprinkled with toasted coconut, alongside cinnamon tostadas.

Fruits and vegetables:

1 ripe pineapple, peeled, cored, and diced (about 3 cups)

½ ripe cantaloupe, peeled, seeded, and diced (about 3 cups)

1 large golden bell pepper, seeded and diced

2 Granny Smith apples, peeled and diced

1 large ripe mango, seeded and diced (1 cup)

2 serranos, minced

Flavorings:

2–3 teaspoons grated fresh ginger

1 teaspoon lemon zest

4 or more tablespoons fresh lime juice

1 cup silver or pineapple-infused tequila (see page 61)

2–3 cups pineapple juice

½ teaspoon freshly ground white pepper

splash citrus syrup (page 42), optional

garnishes: finely chopped jícama, mild chile pepper, lime wedges, slices of star fruit, cinnamon tostadas

Dice all fruits and vegetables by hand and place in a large bowl. Mix all ingredients together and allow to chill for at least 6 hours, or overnight. For a thinner texture, add more pineapple juice. Since the fruits' flavor will vary, taste to adjust the balance of sweet and acidic—add more tequila, citrus syrup, or lime juice as needed.

Makes about 10 cups

Gazpacho Macho
(Gazpacho Laced with Tequila)

There is a pronounced Mexican bravado to this Spanish favorite. It's zesty and refreshing—almost like eating spicy salsa with a spoon. Serve it chilled with shots of ice-cold tequila and pass bowls of condiments: avocado chunks, boiled shrimp, lime wedges, chopped cilantro, and croutons.

4 large, vine-ripened tomatoes (about 2 pounds), seeded and chopped

1 yellow bell pepper, seeded and diced

1 red bell pepper, seeded and diced

3 cloves garlic, minced

2–4 serrano peppers, seeded and minced

2 cucumbers, peeled, seeded, and diced

4 green onions, diced

1 medium white onion, diced

¼ teaspoon whole allspice

½ teaspoon whole black peppercorns

½ teaspoon whole coriander seeds

3 cups tomato juice

3 tablespoons fresh lime juice

1 cup premium silver tequila

3 tablespoons sherry vinegar

3 tablespoons red wine vinegar

4 tablespoons olive oil

1 teaspoon salt

2 tablespoons chopped fresh cilantro

3 tablespoons chopped fresh basil

condiments (optional): avocado chunks, boiled shrimp, lime wedges, chopped green onions, garlic croutons, chopped cilantro and/or basil

Dice vegetables by hand and place in a large bowl. Grind spices in a spice grinder and add to chopped vegetables along with remaining ingredients, whisking in olive oil last. Chill for at least 6 hours or overnight; then, adjust the flavor, adding more vinegar, lime juice, salt, or tequila if needed. Add freshly chopped herbs and serve in chilled bowls accompanied by condiments and shots of tequila.

Makes about 10 cups

¡Que Fresa!
(Summer Strawberry Gazpacho)

Sue Simms, a friend and fabulous cook, created this refreshing recipe to serve on blistering days at her San Angelo ranch. Its rosy and vibrant splash of summertime colors make it a lovely luncheon treat. My addition of a silver tequila enhances the citrus and strawberry flavors. Serve for brunch in chilled crystal goblets garnished with fresh strawberries, accompanied with cinnamon tostadas or as a delightful first course to grilled salmon.

1 quart fresh strawberries, hulled, quartered, and chopped

4 navel oranges, peeled (all white pith removed), sliced, then chopped

½ cup celery, minced

1 large red bell pepper, minced

6 red ripe Roma tomatoes, seeded and chopped

2 fresh red-ripened jalapeños or Fresno peppers, minced

¾ cup silver or strawberry-infused tequila

2 tablespoons fresh lime juice

2 tablespoons balsamic vinegar

2–3 cups freshly squeezed orange juice

2 tablespoons fresh mint, finely chopped

2 teaspoons grated orange zest

½ teaspoon white peppercorns, freshly ground

splash citrus syrup (page 42), optional

salt to taste

garnishes: whole fresh strawberries, cinnamon tostada chips, lime wedges, mint sprigs

Mix all ingredients together and chill for at least 6 hours. Add more fresh orange juice and tequila if a thinner texture is desired. Since fruit varies remarkably in flavor, adjust flavorings to taste to achieve the balance of sweet and tart. Serve in goblets garnished with fresh strawberries accompanied at the table with icy shots of silver tequila and colorful condiments.

Makes about 10 cups

Note: For cinnamon tostada chips, follow recipe on page 116, using flour tortillas. Sprinkle with cinnamon and sugar after frying.

Onion Soup Inolvidable
(Unforgettable Onion Soup)

The lingering sweet and heady aroma of this simmering soup reminds me of the smell of *piñas* baking in the *hornos*. When adding tequila to sauteéing onions, the alcohol burns off, leaving the natural sweetness of the agave to flavor the soup. Serve piping hot and pass the condiments. This makes a great first course or an unforgettable meal.

For the soup:

3 tablespoons butter

2 tablespoons olive oil

2½ pounds yellow onions, thinly sliced

3 medium leeks, washed well and chopped, with some of the green tops

1 cup tequila añejo

2 quarts homemade chicken stock

1 teaspoon dried thyme

1 teaspoon dried oregano

bay leaf

salt and freshly ground white pepper to taste

2 tablespoons red wine vinegar

For the mushroom/poblano sauté:

2 tablespoons butter

1 tablespoon olive oil

4 cloves garlic, minced

6 green onions, chopped

½ pound fresh mushrooms, sliced

4 poblano peppers, roasted, peeled, seeded, and cut into rajas (see page 113)

1 tablespoon añejo tequila

2 tablespoons fresh minced marjoram, thyme, or cilantro

salt and pepper to taste

Garnishes:

8 croutons (page 137)

8 ounces grated Monterey Jack cheese

fresh sprigs of cilantro, marjoram, or thyme

lime wedges

condiments: chopped green onions, lime wedges, and extra croutons

Melt 3 tablespoons butter and 2 tablespoons olive oil in a large pot over medium heat. Add onions and leeks and cook until soft, about 15 minutes. Raise heat to medium-high and continue to cook until onions are caramelized (about 30 minutes), stirring often. Pour in the 1 cup tequila and simmer 5 minutes, to burn off the alcohol. Add the stock, herbs, salt and pepper to taste, and vinegar and continue to simmer for about 30 minutes.

Meanwhile, heat the 2 tablespoons butter and 1 tablespoon olive oil in a medium frying pan and briefly sauté the garlic and green onions; add the mushrooms, rajas, 1 tablespoon tequila, fresh herbs, and salt and pepper to taste, and cook briefly until all of the liquid has been absorbed.

To serve, ladle piping hot broth into bowls. Put about 2 tablespoons of the mushroom-poblano sauté in each bowl, top with a crouton, and sprinkle with Monterey Jack cheese. Garnish with fresh herbs and serve with lime wedges and shots of tequila.

Serves 8

Pedro's Pumpkin Soup
(Creamy Pumpkin Soup with Ancho-Tequila Butter)

This hearty, flavorful harvest soup shows off New World treasures and vibrant colors: pumpkin, chiles, and golden tequila. Serve each bowl with a dollop of brick-red ancho-tequila butter, or a generous sprinkling of grated white cheese. With cornbread muffins and a salad, this makes a filling autumn meal.

The soup:

4 tablespoons butter
2 tablespoons olive oil
2 medium yellow onions, chopped
3 leeks, washed well and chopped with some of the green tops
3 cloves garlic, minced
2 jalapeños, minced (optional)
1 large red pepper, chopped
2 carrots, grated
2 bay leaves
1 teaspoon salt

1 can (29 ounces) unsweetened pumpkin
3 whole ancho peppers, stemmed, seeded, and cut into strips
¼ teaspoon whole allspice
½ teaspoon whole white peppercorns
⅛ teaspoon whole cloves
1 teaspoon thyme
2 teaspoons dried marjoram (more if using fresh)
6 cups rich chicken broth
3 or more teaspoons brown sugar
½ cup or more tequila reposado
garnishes: small bowls of one or more of the following: chopped green onions, cilantro, toasted pumpkin seeds, Tequila-Ancho Butter, ancho chile powder, grated Jack cheese

In a heavy soup pot, sauté onions, leeks, garlic, and jalapeños in the butter and olive oil until onions are translucent. Add the red bell pepper, grated carrot, bay leaves, and salt and cook another 5 minutes. Add the pumpkin, herbs and spices, ancho strips, and broth and bring to boil; reduce heat and simmer partially covered for 40 minutes, stirring occasionally. Add brown sugar and tequila, salt and pepper to taste, and simmer 10 minutes. This is best made several hours in advance; soup will thicken as it cools (thin with additional broth as necessary).

Serves 8

Tequila-Ancho Butter

This butter can be made several days in advance, and may be frozen. Try it on corn, squash, muffins, potatoes. In a small bowl, mix together:

1 stick unsalted butter, softened
2 cloves garlic, minced
2 teaspoons toasted ground chile ancho or mild pure chile powder
1 tablespoon reposado tequila
¼ teaspoon salt

Garlicky Croutons
with Parmesan and Crushed Red Chile

1 day-old baguette or 4 bolillos (Mexican crusty rolls)
¼ cup butter
2 tablespoons olive oil
2–3 cloves garlic, minced
½ teaspoon crushed dried red chile
¼ cup grated Parmesan, (optional)
1 teaspoon pure chile powder (optional)

Preheat oven to 325°F. Slice bread into ½-inch slices. Melt butter with olive oil, garlic, and crushed chile in a small saucepan; brush on bread slices. Place oiled slices on a baking sheet and bake until crisp and golden, about 20 minutes, turning once. Then, if you wish, put croutons in a small bag with the Parmesan and chile powder and shake to coat. Store in an airtight container (they'll keep for several days); reheat before serving.

"maría"
Lady of the night
painted papier mâché
doll with moveable limbs
Celaya,
Guanajuato

ESTRELLAS (Star Attractions)

Part of the fun of party fare is its presentation. A bottle of tequila frozen in a block of ice or a punch bowl brimming with surprises will surely animate conversation. Likewise, dishes that are accompanied by bowls of festive garnishes and condiments inspire creativity and encourage guests to participate in making their own meal.

I like to have fun at my parties so I serve food that may be made in advance, freeing me to mingle with my guests. The following recipes are colorful, and flavorful, designed especially with tequila drinking in mind!

Chiles en Serapes
(Tequila-Marinated Sirloin Wrapped around Roasted Peppers)

Mexicans sometimes wrap woven cotton or wool *serapes* (blanket-like shawls) around their shoulders for warmth. In this recipe, tender tequila-marinated sirloin (or boneless chicken breasts) wrap around whole roasted green chile peppers stuffed with grated Jack cheese and chopped onions. Quickly seared on both sides, the tender meat is enhanced by the piquant flavor of the roasted pepper and creamy melted cheese.

Instead of hamburgers, serve Chiles en Serapes sandwiched between toasted halves of bolillos (crusty rolls) spread with guacamole at your next outdoor gathering. For a more elegant presentation, serve accompanied by Barco de Oro mounded in a corn husk boat (page 126).

Roast chiles, marinate meat, and grate cheese several hours in advance so that only last-minute cooking is required. This recipe may be assembled several hours before serving and stored covered in the refrigerator until you're ready to grill.

3 New York strip steaks (approximately ¾ pound each), well trimmed, butterflied, split, then lightly pounded

For the rub:

4 cloves garlic, minced
2 green onions, finely chopped
½ teaspoon freshly ground cumin
¼ teaspoon freshly ground pepper
1 dried chile de árbol, ground (optional)
2 teaspoons pure mild chile powder
½ teaspoon salt
1 tablespoon reposado tequila

For the marinade:

2 tablespoons reposado tequila
2 tablespoons red wine vinegar
1 tablespoon fresh lime juice
2 tablespoons cilantro, finely chopped
2 tablespoons olive oil
salt and pepper to taste

For the chiles:

6 New Mexico or Anaheim peppers, roasted and peeled with stems left intact (see page 113)
1 cup grated queso blanco or Monterey Jack
4 green onions, chopped

In a small bowl, mix garlic, onions, spices, chile, and salt; drizzle in tequila to form a paste. Divide the rub evenly among the 6 pieces of steak, rubbing onto both sides with the back of a spoon.

Whisk together the ingredients for the marinade. Put meat in a glass dish, add marinade, and chill for at least 1 hour, or overnight, turning occasionally.

Carefully make a slit in each roasted chile and remove some of the seeds; stuff with about 2 tablespoons grated cheese and ⅙ of the chopped green onions. Fold a piece of steak over each chile, leaving the stem and the tip of the chile exposed. Broil chiles under a preheated broiler 4 inches from the flame, or grill on hot coals for about 3 minutes each side. Serve immediately.

Serves 6

Note: Using *Rancho Mesilla* frozen (vacuum-packed) green chiles which are already roasted makes this an even easier recipe; simply thaw and slip off the charred skins (see Resources). Try substituting 6 boneless, skinless chicken breast halves for the steak. Wrap them around the chiles and broil, seam side down, for 3 minutes; turn and cook until done.

Pollo Enchilado en Salsa Borracha
(Roasted Chicken in Drunken Chile Sauce)

This chile-roasted chicken is rubbed with Salsa Borracha (page 123) and stuffed with oranges, onions and fresh herbs. It is rich, moist, and succulent. Carve it at the table (hot or cold) or take it along on a picnic. You can shred Pollo Enchilado from the bone to use in tacos, salads, or sandwiches. For a fiesta, mound the shredded chicken on a platter with bowls of assorted salsas.

For the chicken:

1 whole chicken, 3½–4 pounds
⅓ cup Salsa Borracha (page 123)
½ teaspoon whole cumin seeds
3–4 cloves garlic, cut into slivers
a generous handful of fresh oregano, marigold mint, marjoram, and/or thyme sprigs
1 white onion, cut into wedges
1 orange, cut into eighths
2 whole dried red chiles colorados or guajillos
salt and freshly ground pepper to taste

Preheat oven to 450°F. Rinse chicken and pat dry. Rub Salsa Borracha generously inside cavity of chicken and under skin, then lightly all over. Insert cumin seeds, garlic slivers, and some of the herb sprigs under the skin of the chicken. Stuff remaining herb sprigs, orange and onion wedges, and the whole chiles in the cavity. Sprinkle the chicken with salt and freshly ground pepper.

Place on a foil-lined baking pan in the middle of the oven; reduce heat to 350°F. Bake for about 1 hour, basting every 15 minutes (you can add a splash of tequila to the pan juices as you baste), until the chicken is tender.

*Serves 4 as an entree,
8–10 shredded as an appetizer*

Note: To prevent irritation from the chiles, wrap your hand in a plastic bag before rubbing the chicken. Turkey or larger roasting chickens may be used in this recipe. You can also stuff a handful of dried fruit into the cavity.

Puerco Miel y Mostaza
(Pork Tenderloin in Tequila-Honey Mustard, inspired by and created for my dear friend, Robert Denton)

Tequila really perks up this sweet and tangy marinade/dipping sauce for pork tenderloin. The tenderloin may be served hot or cold, cut into medallions or thinly sliced as an appetizer. Manzanita (page 129), a green apple and cinnamon salsa makes a wonderful condiment.

For the marinade:

2 tablespoons whole grain mustard
2 tablespoons honey
3 tablespoons añejo tequila
1 tablespoon orange juice
2 teaspoons orange zest
¼–½ teaspoon crushed dried red chile
¼ teaspoon freshly ground allspice
⅛ teaspoon freshly ground cloves
2 tablespoons peanut oil

For the tenderloin:

2 pork tenderloins, ¾ pound each, well trimmed
3 cloves garlic, minced
2 teaspoons paprika or mild pure chile powder
salt and freshly ground pepper

For the tequila-honey mustard:

4 tablespoons whole grain mustard
2 tablespoons honey
2 tablespoons finely chopped red onion
1 habanero or Scotch Bonnet, seeded and minced
1 teaspoon orange zest
1 tablespoon tequila añejo
1 tablespoon orange juice

Mix all the ingredients for the marinade. Rub the tenderloins with the garlic, paprika, salt, and pepper. Place them in a dish and cover with the marinade, rubbing well into the meat. Marinate 4–24 hours, turning occasionally.

In a small bowl, mix together the ingredients for the tequila honey mustard and set aside.

To cook the tenderloin, scrape away the thick marinade and reserve. Grill meat over hot coals for about 7–8 minutes or under a preheated broiler 4–6 inches from the flame. Turn once and baste with reserved marinade. Cut into medallions and serve (hot or cold) with bowls of tequila-honey mustard and green apple relish.

*Serves 3–4 as an entree,
6–8 as an appetizer*

Salpicón
(Spicy Shredded Marinated Beef)

This dish is a fiesta in itself! The Spanish word *salpicón* comes from the word for "splashing" and indeed, this spicy marinated beef dish is splashed with flecks of color and flavor: chopped tomatoes, red onions, and cilantro, bite-sized cubes of avocado and creamy white cheese, and smoky strips of brick-red chipotle peppers.

Salpicón is ideal for a buffet since guests serve themselves by spooning it onto tostadas or hot corn tortillas. It is easy for the host as it may be made a day ahead and is served at room temperature. Mound on a platter and garnish. Margaritas are a must!

For the spiked chipotles:

1 seven ounce can chipotle peppers in adobo sauce

3 tablespoons tequila reposado

1 tablespoon red wine vinegar

For the beef:

2 pounds flank steak

1 tablespoon olive oil

3 cloves garlic, minced

2 bay leaves

1 white onion, peeled and quartered, each quarter studded with 2 cloves

2 carrots, quartered

½ teaspoon whole cumin seed

½ teaspoon whole peppercorns

¼ teaspoon whole allspice

1 teaspoon oregano

2–3 dried chiles de árbol

½ teaspoon salt

4 cups beef stock

For the marinade:

3–4 cloves garlic, minced

½ teaspoons freshly ground cumin

¼ teaspoon freshly ground peppercorns

1 teaspoon dried oregano

1 tablespoon tequila reposado

2 tablespoons lime juice

2 tablespoons red wine vinegar

½ teaspoon salt

2 or more whole spiked chipotles, chopped

3 tablespoons spiked chipotle sauce

3 tablespoons olive oil

The chopped ingredients:

1 white onion, chopped

½ cup chopped cilantro

½ pound Monterey Jack cheese, cut into ½ inch cubes

6 Roma tomatoes, chopped

fresh lime juice to taste

salt to taste

3 avocados, cut into small cubes and drizzled with fresh lime juice

garnishes: spiked chipotle strips, avocado wedges, red onion rings, yucca blossoms, cilantro sprigs, lime wedges, tostada chips

Prepare the chipotles by mixing them and their adobo sauce, the 3 tablespoons tequila, and the 1 tablespoon red wine vinegar together in a bowl; set aside, stirring occasionally and leaving the whole chipotles intact.

Rinse flank steak and pat dry. In a 3-quart Dutch oven, heat olive oil, then add garlic and brown slightly before adding steak; sear on both sides. Add bay leaves, white onion, carrots, spices, chiles, oregano, and ½ teaspoon salt and cover with the beef stock. Bring to a boil; reduce the heat and simmer gently, turning the meat once, until it will shred with a fork (approximately 1½–2 hours).

Meanwhile, in a small bowl, place garlic, cumin, pepper, oregano, 1 tablespoon tequila, 2 tablespoons lime juice, vinegar, and ½ teaspoon salt. Add 3 tablespoons spiked chipotle sauce and 2 or more of the chipotles, cut into strips. Slowly whisk in the olive oil. Set aside.

When meat is tender, cool slightly (reserve broth for other uses), then cut into 2-inch pieces, removing any fat or membrane, and shred.

Place shredded beef in a large marinating dish with onion, cilantro and cheese. Toss with the marinade; cover and chill for 4–6 hours or overnight, tossing occasionally.

A few hours before serving, add the chopped tomatoes, drizzle with fresh lime juice, add salt to taste and toss gently.

Serve salpicón on a platter, surrounded with the avocado cubes, and garnish it festively. Any remaining spiked chipotle mixture may be served at the table for those desiring an added kick.

Serves 10 or more

Note: Salpicón may be made with boneless shoulder of venison instead of flank steak.

Pescado Margarita
(Fish Margarita-Style)

The essence of a margarita makes a big splash in this colorful, refreshing grilled fish. It's also delicious served cold as a salad on a bed of greens drizzed with Salsa Jardinera (page 122) or alongside Barca de Oro (page 128).

The fish:

4 fresh fish fillets (about ½ pound each), such as halibut, red snapper, amberjack, or mahi mahi, rinsed and patted dry

The marinade:

3 tablespoons fresh lime juice

1 tablespoon Cointreau

3 tablespoons silver tequila

½ cup finely chopped fresh basil

The rub

2 teaspoons orange zest

1 teaspoon lime zest

2 tablespoons minced shallots

2 teaspoons whole coriander seeds, freshly ground

1 teaspoon whole white pepper corns, freshly ground

½ teaspoon crushed dried red chile, optional

½ teaspoon salt

2 tablespoons peanut oil

In a small bowl, mix the ingredients for the marinade and set aside. Combine the ingredients for the rub, (it should form a thick paste) and spread on both sides of the fish fillets.

Place fillets in a glass dish and cover both sides well with the marinade. Refrigerate for 30 minutes, turning once.

Grill or broil until tender. The center should look moist and flaky. Sprinkle fish with fresh lime juice before serving.

Serves 6

Note: Do not overcook the fish; remember, the citrus marinade has already "cooked" it some.

Hoppin' Jalapeño
Carrot Cake

FINALES FABULOSOS
(Fabulous Finales)

Sometimes a snifter of fine añejo or an exotic tequila liqueur (recipes pages 100-102) are delectable desserts in themselves. Other times, you might want more. From an elegant citrus flan to a whimsical carrot cake, tequila shines as an unexpected surprise.

Flan Famoso
(Citrus Flan Flambéed with Tequila)

This is the loviest way to light up a fiesta! Flambé this luscious golden *flan* custard with tequila at the table to delight your guests. Velvety and light, redolent of citrus and spice, it is a sumptuous finale for a spicy Southwestern or Mexican meal. I serve it on a large platter surrounded with halfslices of oranges and lemons arranged in a sunburst fashion. Flan Famoso is exquisite with Ambrosia, a gingered-tequila liqueur (page 101).

1 cup granulated sugar for the caramel, plus 1 cup granulated sugar, preferably vanilla-scented (see page 44)

1 quart half-and-half

zest of three Valencia oranges, without bitter white pith

¼ teaspoon salt

½ teaspoon mace

7 eggs

2 egg yolks

3 tablespoons añejo tequila

2 tablespoons Grand Marnier

½ teaspoon vanilla

garnishes: orange slices, lemon slices, sprigs of lemon-scented herbs

In a heavy two-quart saucepan, heat the sugar for the caramel on low heat until it begins to dissolve. Raise heat and stir gently as sugar caramelizes. When deep golden brown and fluid, pour into a 10-inch by 2-inch baking dish, swirling it around to evenly coat the bottom of the dish and halfway up the sides. Work quickly and carefully with heavy mitts; it is very hot! Set aside on a rack.

In a heavy pan on medium heat, scald half-and-half with orange zest, salt, and mace (filling your kitchen with delightful aromas!). Meanwhile, lightly beat eggs and yolks together in a large bowl along with remaining 1 cup sugar. Gradually add the scalded half-and-half mixture to the egg mixture, stirring gently. Add tequila, Grand Marnier, and vanilla. Strain the whole mixture into the caramelized dish to remove the citrus zest (you may leave some in if you wish) and any egg particles.

Set the flan in a *baño de Maria* (see below). Pour enough hot water to reach halfway up the sides of the flan. Bake in a preheated 325°F oven for about 1½ hours. Flan is ready when a skewer inserted in the middle comes out clean. Remove from the oven, leaving it in the baño de Maria for about 15 minutes; cool before refrigerating overnight.

To unmold, slide a knife around the rim of the flan to loosen it; set dish in a pan of hot water for 30 seconds, then carefully invert onto platter. Use a larger platter with a raised edge to prevent the caramel from spilling (place it on top of the flan dish and invert quickly and carefully). Arrange a circle of orange slices around the edge of the flan, with a circle of half lemon slices on top of them. Insert sprigs of lemon-scented herbs.

In a small, heavy saucepan, barely heat 2 tablespoons of tequila. With lights off, ignite the tequila as you pour it onto the flan.

Serves 10–12

Note: To make a baño de María, set the flan into a larger pan with deep sides (I use a roasting pan) and place it in the oven. Use hot water from a teapot to fill the pan with hot water. Should the water begin to boil as the flan is baking, lower the heat or the flan will be filled with air bubbles.

Toronja y Tequila
(Grapefruit Tequila Chiffon Pie)

Tart and refreshing, this citrus chiffon pie melts in your mouth—an etheral way to end an evening! Or serve it at an elegant luncheon garnished with segments of ruby grapefruit and candied violets. No one can believe that this is a grapefruit pie, or that it has tequila as an ingredient, and there is seldom any left once sliced.

For the crust:

1¼ cups honey graham crackers, finely crushed

2 teaspoons grapefruit zest, coarsely grated, without white pith

1 tablespoon granulated sugar

5 tablespoons butter, melted

For the filling:

1½ cups fresh ruby red grapefruit, unstrained with seeds removed

2 teaspoons coarsely grated grapefruit zest (no white pith)

1 package unflavored gelatin

pinch salt

½ cup sugar plus 2 tablespoons

3 eggs, separated

3 tablespoons premium silver tequila

1 tablespoon fresh lime juice

½ pint whipping cream

2 tablespoons sugar

pinch salt

garnishes: ruby red grapefruit wedges, candied violets or grapefruit peel, flowers

Mix ingredients for crust together in a bowl, then press evenly into sides and bottom of a 9½-inch glass pie pan. Chill for 15 minutes in the refrigerator. Bake in a pre-heated 350°F oven for about 7 minutes. Cool.

Combine grapefruit juice and zest, gelatin, sugar, and salt in a small heavy bottomed saucepan. Stir over medium-low heat to a near boil; remove from heat. Lightly beat egg yolks; spoon several tablespoons of the hot mixture into yolks before returning them to the saucepan. Heat on low for 1 minute, stirring gently. Remove from the heat; add the lime juice and the tequila; mixture should be tart and full-flavored but not sour (more sugar may be added later). Pour into a chilled stainless steel bowl and chill until it starts to set and mounds on a spoon (approximately 1 hour).

In chilled bowl, whip the cream until it forms soft mounds, adding the remaining sugar if desired (depending upon the tartness of the grapefruit mixture). Beat the egg whites with a pinch of salt until stiff peaks form. In a large bowl, fold the whipped cream and the egg whites into the grapefruit mixture and turn into the crust. Chill for at least 6 hours or overnight. Serve on chilled plates. Garnish with ruby red grapefruit segments and/or candied grapefruit peel, fresh herb sprigs, johnny-jump ups, or candied violets.

Serves 8–10

Note: Use only fresh and delicious grapefruit such as Texas Rio Ruby Star or substitute other citrus for the grapefruit such as tangerine or bllod orange, decreasing sugar lightly as needed.

Pastel De Almendras
(Spanish Almond Cake Laced with Tequila Añejo)

This cake, inspired by a Spanish recipe which originally used brandy, resembles a moist pound cake. It is delicious hot out of the oven with coffee at a Sunday brunch. Or serve it for dessert topped with Mexican Whipped Cream, slices of ripe mango, and a dollop of Cliff's Tequila Orange Marmalade (see note).

1 cup plus 2 tablespoons whole almonds, lightly toasted

1 cup all-purpose flour

1½ teaspoons baking powder

¼ teaspoon salt

½ pound unsalted butter

1 cup sugar, preferably vanilla-scented

4 eggs

¼ teaspoon pure almond extract

3 tablespoons tequila añejo

2 teaspoons orange zest

1 teaspoon lemon zest

¼ teaspoon freshly grated nutmeg

garnishes: confectioners' sugar, freshly grated nutmeg, Mexican Whipping Cream, sliced mangos, Cliff's Tequila Orange Marmalade

Finely grind almonds; reserve 2 tablespoons. Mix remaining nuts with flour, baking powder, and salt and set aside.

Cream butter and sugar with an electric mixer. Add the eggs, one at a time, mixing well. blend in the almond extract, tequila, and citrus zests. Mix in almond/flour mixture until incorporated. Spread batter into a 9½-inch by 2-inch pan (or a springform pan) that has been buttered and dusted with flour. Sprinkle with remaining ground almonds. Place in preheated 325°F oven on the middle rack and bake until tester comes out clean (approximately 40-45 minutes). Cool 10 minutes; remove from pan by inverting onto a platter. Sprinkle with confectioners' sugar and freshly grated nutmeg; garnish. Serve with Rompope od a tasty coffee drink.

Serves 8–10

Note: My dear friend and bon vivant, Cliff Alsup, brings me cherished jars of this marmalade: "Cut thick ends from 12 navel oranges and 3 lemons and slice as thin as possible. Measure the cut fruit, and for each 4 cups (packed with juice), add 1 cup water and 2 cups tequila. Let stand overnight. In the morning, bring to a boil and cook until fruit is tender, which may take as long as 2 hours. Measure cooked fruit, and for each cup of fruit, add 1 cup sugar. Cook until sugar is dissolved, then boil rapidly until it gels. Pour into hot sterilized jars and seal." Delicious on toast or muffins, vanilla ice cream, or by the spoonful!

Embroidered cloth Pátzcuaro, Michoacán

"Come on girl give the bottle a whirl. If you won't dance for another I'll prance."

ANDELE COMADRE
BAILE LA BOTELLA
Y SI NO LA BAILA
YO LE DOY CON ELLA

Hoppin' Jalapeño
(Jalapeño Carrot Cake with Tequila/Lime Cream Cheese Frosting)

This dark, dense carrot cake has a tropical flair and is hopping with flavors. And yes, jalapeños are one! They offer flecks of green and a new dimension of spiciness. (You may even find yourself adding another jalapeño each time you make it!) A creamy frosting laced with tequila añejo and lime zest is delicious!

½ cup golden raisins

3 tablespoons tequila añejo or tequila infused with orange peel

2 cups all-purpose flour

2 teaspoons baking powder

1 teaspoon baking soda

1 teaspoon salt

2 teaspoons cinnamon

2 teaspoons ground ginger

3 whole cloves, ground

½ teaspoon whole allspice berries, ground

4 large eggs

1 cup canola oil

1 cup granulated sugar

1 cup dark brown sugar, tightly packed

3 cups grated carrots, tightly packed

1 teaspoon coarsely grated lime zest

2 teaspoons coarsely grated orange zest

3 or more jalapeños, seeded and minced

1 can (8 ounces) unsweetened crushed pineapple, drained

¾ cup Baker's sweetened coconut flakes

For the frosting:

8 ounces cream cheese, softened

4 tablespoons unsalted butter, softened

2 cups confectioners' sugar

2 tablespoons tequila añejo (I use Sauza Conmemorativo)

1 tablespoon Grand Marnier

2 heaping teaspoons grated lime zest

garnishes: fresh flowers such as zinnias, calendulas, or maigolds and fresh herb sprigs pressed into the cake.

Plump raisins in tequila. In a large bowl, sift the flour, baking powder, baking soda, salt, and spices and set aside. In a large bowl, beat eggs until pale yellow, add sugars, then slowly mix in oil. Add the dry ingredients on low speed just until blended. Fold in the carrots, pineapple, raisins, coconut, and jalapeños.

Pour into a buttered and floured 12-cup bundt pan, and bake in a 350°F oven for 55 minutes or until a tester comes out clean. Allow to cool for 10 minutes before removing from pan; cool on a rack. Best made a day in advance of frosting (store at room temperature tightly covered). Once frosted, store in the refrigerator up to 4 days.

To make the frosting: In a bowl, blend cream cheese and butter until smooth. Slowly mix in the sugar, Grand Marnier, tequila, and lime zest until creamy. It will be thinner than most cream cheese frostings so there will be some left over. Frost cake quickly and refrigerate in a covered cake plate. Serve at room temperature, garnishing with the flowers just before serving.

Serves 12

APPENDIX

Tequila for Whatever Ails You

Para todo mal, mezcal.
Para todo bien, también

❋

For all that ails you, mezcal.
For all that's good, as well.

¡Salud! To Your Health

Lázaro Pérez, just like tequila, is a part of Jalisco's colorful history. He ran a *botica* (pharmacy) of grand repute in Guadalajara and was also an historian, an astronomer, a meteorologist, and a biochemist. In 1887, he wrote *Estudio Sobre el Maguey Llamado Mezcal en el Estado de Jalisco*, a comprehensive study on the maguey. Pérez stressed the importance of imbibing tequila in moderation to prevent the immoral consequences of inebriation, and he extolled tequila's virtues.

Pérez advocated tequila's benefit as a general tonic, a diuretic, a digestif, an antiseptic for wounds, and a poultice for inflammatory aches and pains. He stated that tequila eases hunger, quenches thirst, stimulates the appetite, gives vigor and longevity to the aged, calms respiratory distress, and diminishes the depression of poverty. He also claimed that tequila enlivens the intelligence, prevents boredom, and procures pleasant illusions! (No wonder I like it!)

Señor Pérez suggested that the weak or the aged may prefer to dilute their tequila with water and sugar or drink it as a tea, sweetened and flavored with anise or cinnamon.

A Shot a Day Keeps the Doctor Away?

Tequila is believed by many Mexicans to have effects as an aphrodisiac, an after-shave, and an antiseptic, as well as a blood purifier and a cure for venereal disease. Mexican women have told me that they rub it on the gums of their teething babes and sip tequila during labor to ease the pain and to "gain strength."

Today, many Mexicans, especially those living in rural areas, still drink tequila as a panacea for anything that ails them, and as a preventive measure as well. Some sip several shots a day: one in the late morning (as a stimulant and apéritif), one with the midday meal (as a digestif), and one before bed. They imbibe tequila for what they believe to be its restorative and curative purposes, not just for inebriation, treasuring both the invigorating and the soothing spirit of the agave.

Tequila is to many Mexicans what wine is to the French and Italians and sherry is to the Spanish: a natural part of life, an enjoyment worth savoring. Instead of guzzling several drinks in rapid succession during the "cocktail hour," many of them savor their libations in a moderate and leisurely fashion.

Tequila need not be slugged down in numerous shots, although some seem to think so; instead, it may be sipped slowly in reverence of its virtues.

Remember, moderation is always the best medicine!

Tequila en un jarro
para el catarro.

✦

Tequila in a jar
for the catarrh.

Para Catarro
(For a Cough)

My friend Javier Aviles made this tasty *té de limón* ("lime tea") for me when I was stricken with the flu. It helped me feel better (or not feel the pain), soothed my cough, and helped me sleep. This recipe is for two: one for the patient, one for the nurse.

3 cups water
1 small handful fresh citrus leaves
1 three-inch piece of cinnamon, crushed
Peel of ½ lime (without bitter white pith)
4 ounces gold tequila
1 juicy lime, cut in half
4 teaspoons honey
Ground cayenne to taste

Bring water to boil in a small saucepan, along with citrus leaves, cinnamon, and lime peel; reduce heat and simmer on medium heat for about 10 minutes until it turns a rich golden color. Meanwhile, in each mug place 2 teaspoons of honey, the juice of half the lime, 2 ounces tequila, and cayenne to taste. Stir well to dissolve honey. Pour in enough of the cinnamon/citrus tea to fill each mug. *¡Salud!*

Note: when fresh citrus leaves are not available, use more lime peel and add some freshly squeezed lime juice to the simmering tea. I like to use commercially available cayenne-flavored honey; sometimes, however, I simply crush a chile pequín in the mug with the honey instead of using the cayenne.

Makes 2 servings

Damiana Love Tonic

The population of Mexico seems to be prolific enough without the aid of aphrodisiacs; however, tequila and damiana, a pungent and aromatic herb (page 71), are two notorious ones, which I have combined in a spirited love potion. Imbibe before bedtime. At the least, it may inspire sweet dreams.

1½ ounces dried damiana leaves (available in herbal and health food stores)
Peel of 1 orange cut in a continual spiral
1 pint silver tequila
½–¾ cup citrus syrup (page 42)

In a glass bottle, infuse damiana and orange peel in tequila for a week, shaking daily. Strain through paper coffee filters, discarding damiana leaves. Sweeten to taste, adding 1 tablespoon syrup at a time (I like it slightly bitter). Store in a cool, dark place. Some sediment may settle.

Makes about a pint

Cruda, La Cruz, Descompuesto
"Raw," "The Cross," "Broken": Hung Over!

In Mexico, salt, lime, and plenty of chiles or another shot of tequila seem to be a ubiquitous prescription for the ill effects suffered the morning after too much drinking. Trading one pain for another seems to be the best Mexican remedy for a hangover: *un clavo saca otro clavo*. The new form of pain may come from another drinking bout, a bite into a searing serrano, or any morsel doused in a fiery *salsa picante*. Sweating, screaming, and swearing are requisite accompaniments. When I once asked an elderly Mexican man what to do to relieve a hangover, he chuckled, "Si trais una cruda, ponte otra borrachera." (If you have a hangover, get drunk again.)

Some recommend a cup of hot tea, especially *yerbanís* (Mexican mint marigold), *estafiate* (artemisia) or *herba buena* (mint). Others suggest freshly squeezed orange juice spiced with chiles, or a tall glass of sparkling mineral water sprinkled liberally with salt and lots of fresh lime juice. Fresh papaya, liberally doused with fresh lime juice and sprinkled with salt and chile powder, is another purported cure, especially to ease gastric distress.

Para una buena cruda
otra buena borrachera.

For a bad hangover
It's best to start over.

Mexicans use the picturesque name *levanta muertos* (raise the dead) to describe perky edible remedies purported to cure the hangover. Any variety of tongue-searing *salsas picosas* (or drinks or dishes peppered with them) may be called by that name. *Huevos rancheros*, fried eggs served on a softened corn tortilla smothered in salsa picante, is one such "morning after" favorite. However, two of the most traditional hangover remedies are *menudo*, a spicy soup, and *vuelve a la vida*, a picante seafood cocktail. Ceviche (fresh fish or shellfish marinated in lime juice) and other seafood concoctions are also sometimes called vuelve a la vida.

CENTZONTOTOCHTIN

Four Hundred Rabbits and the Diverse Forms of Intoxication

In his chronicles of pre-Hispanic life, Franciscan Fray Bernardino Sahagún cited in *The Diverse Manners of Drunks*, the four hundred consequences of intoxication. These consequences were influenced by the 400 rabbit dieties. Although Sahagún wrote in the sixteenth century, the manners of drunks do not seem to have changed much today. (Blame it on the rabbits!)

Menudo
Tripe Soup

Many North Americans may rather suffer the ill-fated consequences of a hangover than to even consider swallowing spoonfuls of a spicy soup made from the lining of a cow's stomach (*panzita* or tripe) and calf's feet. But cantinas, restaurants and late-night street vendors throughout northern Mexico serve bowls of menudo (especially during the weekends) for those who have imbibed more than they wished.

Chopped onions, cilantro, oregano, and wedges of lime as well as a fiery salsa made from chile de árbol or pequín always accompany the steaming bowls of this rich chile-flavored broth filled with tender chunks of honeycomb tripe. Pozole (hominy) is an optional addition. Menudo has become a weekend specialty in restaurants north of the border as well, better in some places than in others. Making it at home assures quality ingredients and freshness.

2 calf's feet, split in half lengthwise, then crosswise, well washed (optional)

2 onions, quartered

2 bay leaves

6 quarts water

5 pounds honeycomb tripe with fat shaved off, cut into ¾-inch pieces; soaked and rinsed thoroughly several times

8–10 ancho chiles

¼ pound guajillo chiles

6–8 cloves garlic, minced

1 teaspoon marjoram

2 teaspoons oregano

1 teaspoon thyme

½ teaspoon cumin

5 leaves epazote, optional

2 cans (15 ounces) hominy, rinsed (optional)

Salt to taste

Garnishes: chopped white onion, chopped serranos or whole chiles pequines, chopped cilantro, dried oregano, lime wedges, hot salsas

Place calf's feet, onion, and bay leaves in a large stock pot; add water. Bring to a boil, and simmer uncovered on medium heat for 1½ hours, occasionally skimming the foam. Strain and reserve the stock.

Return strained stock to the pot, along with the cooked calf's feet and tripe, and bring to boil; reduce heat and simmer for about 3 or 4 hours, or until tripe is almost tender. Do not boil or tripe may toughen. Then, if desired, separate the meat from the bone of the calf's foot, discarding the gristle, skin, and bone; otherwise, the meat may later be eaten from the bone from the soup bowl.

While tripe is cooking, remove stem and seeds from the dried chiles and soak in hot water to cover for 15 minutes. In a blender, grind chiles with garlic and enough of the soaking water to form a slightly thickened sauce; set aside.

Add chile sauce to tripe soup and bring to a boil, along with the spices and the salt; reduce heat and simmer the last 30 minutes it is cooking, or until the tripe is tender. If desired, add hominy and epazote during the last 15 minutes, with additional salt to taste. Serve piping hot with the garnishes and a basket of hot tortillas.

Note: Tripe must be very fresh (crystal white) and well washed. Calf's feet are now readily available (often frozen) in Southwestern grocery stores; pig's feet may be substituted.

Serves whoever will eat it!

"Changos"
Brightly painted
black clay monkeys
in straw hats...
filled with
mezcal!
Oaxaca,
Mexico

Menudo
para el crudo.

❋

*Menudo
for the hangover.*

Vuelve a la Vida
(Spicy Seafood Cocktail)

In the *palapas* (thatch-roofed restaurants) on the beach in Mexico, waiters serve this medley of *mariscos* (seafood) in tall soda fountain glasses with spoons. I serve it instead, in wide-mouthed margarita glasses with green cactus stems, colorfully combining the fresh pink shrimp with chunks of avocado, freshly chopped onion, tomatoes, and cilantro in a spicy cocktail sauce. Cooks in Yucatán and Campeche drizzle smoky chipotle salsa over the top, but I prefer to drizzle it with chile pepper-flavored tequila, a fitting *levanta muertos*. Accompanied with a sparkling Margarita Collins (page 73), how could you help but come to life?

2 pounds fresh medium shrimp, boiled/seasoned (do not overcook!), peeled, and de-veined

2 medium tomatoes, chopped
1 small white onion
3 or more serranos, chopped
½ cup fresh cilantro, chopped
12 ounces premium quality homestyle seafood cocktail sauce
Juice of 4 Mexican limes
½ cup or more chile pepper-flavored tequila
your favorite bottled hot sauce to taste
Salt and freshly ground white pepper to taste
3 avocados, peeled, seeded, and cubed
Lime wedges
garnishes: thin strips of canned chipotle peppers (optional)

Mix together the ingredients except for the avocado. Chill for 1–2 hours. Adjust the seasonings and gently toss in the avocado cubes.

Note: Fresh oysters, steamed clams, crabmeat, and/or squid may be used for part of the shrimp.

Serves 6–8

Torito
(Little Bull)

During fiestas in his hometown of Luvianos, Mexico, Javier Aviles and his amigos make a lively drink. They squeeze the juice from the oranges and the limones growing nearby, spike it with *mucho* tequila, season it with finely chopped chile peppers and onions, and add a good splash of beer to give it some fizz. Sounds like this may cure a hangover before it happens.

This may sound rather wild, but it is surprisingly tasty: reminiscent of Mexico's renowned pico de gallo—a colorful and refreshing medley of orange segments, jicama chunks, chopped red onions, and serrano peppers marinated in tart lime juice and dusted with bright-red chile powder. Toritos make a delightful alternative for Bloody Marys for brunch.

6 cups freshly squeezed orange juice
1 cup freshly squeezed lime juice
2 cups silver tequila (partial chile-pepper-flavored tequila if desired)
1 teaspoon salt
1 Mexican beer (12 ounces)
2 serrano peppers (or more, to taste), preferably red-ripened, finely chopped
¼ cup red onion, finely chopped

In a glass pitcher, mix together the citrus juices, tequila, salt, and serranos; chill for several hours. Before serving, add beer and sprinkle with onions. Serve in tall glasses over ice (try festive ice cubes with chile peppers, or chile pepper flowers hooked over the rim of the glass (see page 47).

Serves 6–8

A day without tequila is a day you will remember

—*Robert del Grande, chef-owner Cafe Annie, Houston*

Toro Bravo
Brave Bull (Bullshot)

Fellow tequila enthusiast and dear friend Mark Mattingly and I have sampled many tequilas together. His secret for the morning after? A good dose of homemade beef bouillon spiked with chipotle-flavored tequila, a sure-fire way to wake you up!

2 ounces peppered tequila (preferably chipotle-flavored)
5 ounces homemade beef bouillon
Dash of Worcestershire sauce
Freshly cracked pepper
Lime wedge

Fill a glass beaker with ice. Add peppered tequila and remaining ingredients and stir until chilled. Strain into a highball glass with ice and a squeeze of fresh lime juice.

Note: Experiment with different flavors of chile pepper-flavored tequila (page 64). For a special treat, use pepper ice cubes (page 47). For a change, substitute 3 ounces of clam juice and 2 ounces of tomato juice for the bouillon.

Serves 1

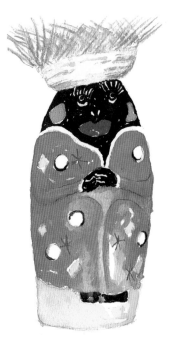

RESOURCES

*No hay mal
que por bien no venga.*

*Nothing bad happens
that good will not follow.*

Coyote Cocina
800-866-HOWL

Southwestern catalog featuring chiles, spices, salsas, coffees, and cookware.

Daum Cristal France
Evelyn Drefus
694 Madison Ave.,
New York, NY 10021

212-355-2060

An assortment of cacti in hues of celadon and amber form the stems and the stoppers for the decanters in the exquisite Pâte de Verre " Cactus Collection"; also a cobalt and shimmering gold agave-inspired perfume bottle titled "TEQUILA" from the "Arguments of Desire Collection", all designed for Daum by Hilton McConnico.

Dazey Corporation
One Dazey Circle,
Industrial Airport,
KS 66031

800-255-6120

Dazey Stripper strips the peel from citrus in a continuous spiral.

Don Alfonso Foods
José C. Marmolejo
P.O. Box 201988
Austin, TX 78720-1988

800-456-6100;
fax 800-765-7373

Authentic Mexican chiles, herbs, spices, utensils, salsa, books. Catalog $1, refunded with puchase.

El Paso Chile Company
909 Texas Ave,
El Paso, TX 79901

800-27-IS HOT

Southwestern specialty products, salsas, chiles and spices, gifts.

India Tree Gourmet Spices and Specialties
Gretchen Goehrend
4240 Gilman Place West #B,
Seattle, WA 98199

800-369-4848;
fax 206-282-0587

Sparkling sugar crystals, in fiesta colors, to rim glasses.

Mozzarella Company
2914 Elm Street,
Dallas, TX 75226,

800-798-2954

Hand-made Mexican cheeses, some flavored with herbs and chiles.

Pegasus Coffee Company
Austin, TX

800-598-2788

Estate grown coffees available in colorful handwoven bags reflective of native Guatemalan Indian culture.

Rancho Mesilla
Stuart Hutson
P.O. Box 39,
Mesillas, NM 88046

505-525-2266

Frozen vacuum-packed flame-roasted New Mexico chiles, sun-dried chiles, pecans.

Reed's Jamaican-Style Ginger Brew and Spiced Apple Brew
22060 Ybarra Road,
Woodland Hills, CA 91364

800-99-REEDS

Sazaki Company
Sasaki's "Stone Collection" by Soichiro Sasakura includes a sleek, handblown crystal shot glass with an ebony base that resembles a pebble—a beautiful accent for the Southwestern table. Dan Chelsea's "Martini Chiller", another contemporary crystal design consists of a clear crystal cone nesting in a clear crystal sphere, which can be filled with ice to keep tequila icy cold.

212-686-5080 for information about retailers in your area

Toddy Products, Inc.
Toddy Coffee Maker
1206 Brooks Street.
Houston, Tx 77009

713-225-2066

cold-brew coffee maker, coffee.

GRACIAS

A los mezcaleros y los tequileros,
a los cantineros y los cocineros,
a los mariachis y los artesanos
y para mis memorias de Mexico...
les doy mis gracias.

To the agave field workers and the distillery owners,
to the bartenders and the cooks,
to the mariachis and the folk artists,
and for my memories of Mexico...
I give my thanks.

My sincere appreciation to all those who made ¡TEQUILA! a reality. Those generous souls from both sides of the border have my heartfelt gracias for their information and inspiration. Thanks to all those involved with the production of this book: to John Harrisson, my agent: to Ten Speed Press for the opportunity to share with others my love of Mexico; to Marsia Reese for her editorial help in the early stage of the project; to Mariah Bear, managing editor, for her enthusiasm; to Victor Guerra, for his poetic translation of the *dichos*; and to Frauke Baylor of Blue Trout Catering, for testing the recipes.

Special thanks to Julie Marshall for her charming and colorfull illustrations and deepest gratitude to Fifth Street Design in Berkeley—Brent Beck, Jerry Meek, and Torri Randall—who so lovingly captured the spirt of Mexico in the pages of this book.

Muchísimas gracias to Tomás Gilliland and Miguel Ravago, my ever-gracious *padrinos*, whose glorious Fonda San Miguel Restaurant provided the background for the backcover photograph with Mariachi Estrella shot by Bill Records in Austin, Texas.

I also thank my parents, Patricia and Stuart Hutson who have always encouraged my travels and tales; and Moondance, Mayahuel, and the magical maguey . . .

... y a mis queridos amigos,
un brindis.

and to many dear friends,
I raise my glass.

BIBLIOGRAPHY

Baker, Charles Jr. *The Gentleman's Companion*. New York: Crown Publishers, 1946.

Barrios, Virginia B. *A Guide to Tequila, Mezcal, and Pulque*. Mexico D. F. : Minutiae Mexicana, S. A., 1988.

Castaños, Dr. Roman Serra, (Director General de Normas), et al. *"Norma Oficinal Mexicana "Tequila."* Mexico D. F. : March 31, 1978.

Copper, Brad. "The Man Who Invented the Margarita." *Texas Monthly Magazine*, 1974.

Corn, Elaine. "Margarita Man." *Chile Pepper Magazine*, Sept/Oct 1992. Colen, Bruce David. "Tequila." *Town and Country*, June 1988.

Curtis, Gregory. "The Truth About Tequila." *Texas Monthly Magazine*, September 1975.

Farga, Amando. *Historia de la Comida en Mexico*. Mexico D. F. : Lithografica Mexico, S. A.., 1980.

Corman, Marion, and Alba, Felipe P. *The Tequila Book*. Chicago: Contemporary Books, Inc., 1978.

Guerrero, Raúl. *El Pulque*. Mexico D. F. : Editorial Joaquin Mortiz, S. A., 1985.

Jones, Stan. *Cooking with Tequila Sauza*. Los Angeles: Bar Guide Enterprizes, 1979.

Lima, Oswaldo Goncalves de. *El Maguey y el Pulque en los Codices Mexicanos*. Mexico D. F. : Fondo de Cultura Economica, 1986.

Mason, Charles T., and Mason, Patricia B. *A Handbook of Mexican Roadside Flora*. Tucson, Arizona: The University of Arizona Press, 1987.

Novo, Salvador. *Cocina Mexicana*. Mexico D. F. : Editorial Porrua, S. A. , 1976.

Pacult, F. Paul. *"Tequila Rising."* Connoisseur, October 1991.

Pérez, Lázaro. *"Estudio Sobre el Maguey Llamado Mezcal en el Estado de Jalisco." Programa de Estudios Jaliscienses Instituto del Tequila, A. C.* Guadalajara, Jalisco, 1990.

Pla, Rosa, and Tapia, Jesús. *El Agave de las Mieles al Tequila*. Mexico D. F. : Instituto Frances de America Latin, 1990.

Swain, Roger. *"Agaves in the Southwest." Horticulture Magazine*, November, 1987.

Thompson, Helen. *"Barroom Brawl." Texas Monthly Magazine*, July, 1991.

Tunnell, Curtis and Madrid, Enrique. *"Making and Taking Sotol in Chihuahua and Texas". Third Symposium on Resources in the Chihuahuan Desert Region, United States, and Mexico, (published by the Chihuahuan Desert Research Institute*, Alpine, Texas, November 1990.

Weston, Edward. *The Daybooks of Edward Weston*. New York: An Aperture Book, 1973.

Zamora, Rogelio Luna. *La Historia del Tequila*. Mexico D. F. : Consejo Nacional para la Cultura y las Artes, 1991.

INDEX